£2.50

In tune with yourself
children writing poetry –
a handbook for teachers

Jennifer Dunn
Morag Styles
Nick Warburton

To write is for all the world like humming a song – be
but in tune with yourself ... 'tis no matter how high or
how low you take it.

Lawrence Sterne

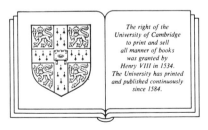

The right of the
University of Cambridge
to print and sell
all manner of books
was granted by
Henry VIII in 1534.
The University has printed
and published continuously
since 1584.

CAMBRIDGE UNIVERSITY PRESS
Cambridge
New York   New Rochelle   Melbourne   Sydney

This book is dedicated to the children with whom the authors
have worked over the years. We are particularly grateful to those
whose poems have been included.

Published by the Press Syndicate of the University of Cambridge
The Pitt Building, Trumpington Street, Cambridge CB2 1RP
32 East 57th Street, New York, NY 10022, USA
10 Stamford Road, Oakleigh, Melbourne 3166, Australia

© Cambridge University Press 1987

First published 1987

Printed in Great Britain at the University Press, Cambridge

British Library cataloguing in publication data
Dunn, Jennifer
In tune with yourself: children writing poetry: a handbook for
teachers.
1. Poetics – Study and teaching – Great Britain 2. English
literature – Study and teaching – Great Britain
I. Title II. Styles, Morag III. Warburton, Nick
808.1 PN1101

ISBN 0 521 33126 9 hard covers
ISBN 0 521 33734 8 paperback

Contents

Introduction

This book sets out to do two things. It sets out to say *why* poetry is an important part of the curriculum, worthy of a teacher's serious consideration. It also sets out to say *how* poetry may be tackled in the classroom.

It does not offer quick and easy ways of casting a net into a sea of children's minds and coming up with a rich haul of poems. Neither does it promise to provide fool-proof formulae for imparting a linguistic ability which will dazzle parents, school inspectors and colleagues alike. Of course, we do believe that anyone who adopts approaches similar to those set out here, and who is prepared to put in the necessary work, will notice an improvement in the quality of the children's writing. He will also have the undoubted pleasure of reading some excellent poems as a result. However, our aims really go further than that. We are more concerned with the processes involved in writing poetry than in any obvious end-product.

In tune with yourself is, therefore, not so much an instruction manual ('First choose your rhymes . . . ') as a guide to the territory you are likely to encounter, with some advice on how to overcome certain natural hazards and get the best from the scenery.

Although three of us combined to write this book, we didn't want it to sound like the proceedings of some anonymous committee. We therefore divided the material between us and went away to write our own sections, reconvening to compare notes and to revise. This means that, to a certain extent, each chapter is idiosyncratic and written in the first rather than the third person. This approach proved to be more than just a nicer way of writing. It also enabled us to view the book from three distinct but complementary viewpoints: those of the teacher, the writer and the educationalist.

The practising teacher is engaged in a day-to-day struggle to implement an increasingly complex curriculum, to find a balance between what is worthwhile and what is merely expedient, and to maintain a freshness when the many demands of the job so often leave one feeling stale. The writer's daily struggle is with words and ideas and how they can be made to count; whether a thing is worth saying or not, and how best to say it. The educationalist is concerned to promote clear aims and good practice among those setting out to teach. (In fact, since one of us is also an anthologist, we can reasonably add a fourth point of view: that of one who cares about the variety of poetic experience available to children.)

The best teachers share with the best writers a single-mindedness, an openness to possibility and a passion for detail. Both teachers and writers need time and the right conditions to develop fully. *In tune with yourself* has been written with this in mind. It has also been written with a love for poetry and a strong belief in teaching as a creative activity and in children as writers.

Note: We have written this book on the basis of our teaching experience in England and have therefore referred to the children's ages in terms commonly used in schools there. These are:

first year juniors	7–8
second year juniors	8–9
third year juniors	9–10
fourth year (top) juniors	10–11

Throughout the book, we have used 'he' to refer to the teacher and 'she' to refer to the pupil.

1 Some preliminary considerations

During my time as a teacher I felt that creative writing was one of the more worthwhile activities to undertake with a class but I would have been hard pressed to say exactly why. I also knew the *sort* of thing I was looking for in children's writing, and thought I could recognise a 'good' piece of work when I saw it. However, there were, I'm sure, 'good' pieces which I failed to recognise, and the question of how to get the children to produce them remained largely unanswered.

It wasn't difficult to see the reason behind this vagueness, these good intentions coupled with uncertainty about where I was going and how to get there. I did not have enough time to think properly about the matter. Many other calls on my teaching time prevented me from giving due consideration to creative writing, either in perspective or detail. As a consequence it remained a frustrating business of hit-and-miss. On some occasions I sensed that the children *did* grow through what they wrote, but on others their efforts, and my efforts on their behalf, seemed diffuse and at best approximate.

Ironically, it was when I gave up teaching to concentrate on my own writing that I was able to find the time to bring these matters into sharper focus and see how much better directed our creative writing sessions could have been.

Consider an evening's marking. Thirty or so poems on the theme of monsters. Among the pile of papers before me I hope to encounter vivid descriptions, stirring narrative, some original and telling phrases. In short, I look for evidence that the children have been inspired. By the time I have looked through the poems I am disappointed and I don't quite know how to respond to their efforts.

What has gone wrong? Perhaps a consideration of the poems themselves will reveal something. They appear to fall into five broad categories:

1. **Poems that work:** *some* of the poems show signs of imaginations fired and language which has been brought to bear on the subject in a thoughtful and exciting way. There are not, however, very many of them.

2. **Poems which seem a lot like one another:**

> Clumping heavily through the night.
> Eyes like fire, voice like the sound of a fog warning.
> The monster comes my way . . .

This seems to have some promise until I realize that several poems from the pile describe the same thing in similar ways. 'He clumps along on heavy feet', one writes. 'Here come his heavy, clumping feet', says another. These, and several others like them, are lines which are not without merit but they have been put together with words and expressions which cropped up in the discussion the class had before they set about writing. Some of the words were even written up on the board. The authors of these poems have shown an ability to recall words and use them in the correct context. In some cases they have shown that they can co-operate with a partner. These things were not, however, what I was looking for. The children whose poems fall into the category exercised more touching obedience than creative thought.

3. **Poems which try to rhyme:** the children whose poems belong to this category concerned themselves more with the fact that they were asked to write a poem than they did with the subject matter which was supposed to stimulate them. I asked, specifically, for a poem. A poem, they reasoned, is something that rhymes. The result is:

> I saw the monster come over the hill.
> I had such a fright I had to swallow a pill.

or:

> The monster's face is horrible and green.
> It looks just like a bean.

4. **Poems which don't get very far:**

> I can see a monster.
> It is very big.
> It has a green head.
> The end.

For some children, a poem like this may represent a considerable effort. It is possible, though, that the effort might have had a little more flesh to it if they had been asked for 'sentences' or 'thoughts' rather than a poem. Most children, on the other hand, are capable of more and better than this. Here they seem to have run up against a vast blank wall. Perhaps all manner of wierd monsters dart and caper on the other side of it but these children have been unable to see them or trap them with words.

5. **Poems which try to be something else:**

> The monster is very frightening.
> He makes me shake like a jelly.
> He has a fearsome mouth.
> The monster is bigger than a house ...

This poem doesn't want to be about the monster but about the fear its author feels at the thought of the monster. I would be happy enough if she forgot my instructions to write about the monster and developed her own more vivid ideas instead. 'He has a fearsome mouth' seems promising. Unfortunately, though, I asked for a poem about monsters and, with the fourth line, I can see her returning dutifully if dully to the task in hand. Her impulse to write is not matched by the instruction she has been given.

What is the reason for this patchy collection from a class of children who think, feel and have their own vital language to employ? Did the lesson itself go wrong?

At the time everything seemed to be ordered well enough. The children attended and responded to questions and comments about monsters. They had been working on Greek myths, so the idea of monsters was not unfamiliar to them. They listened carefully to a recording of 'In the Hall of the Mountain King' from Grieg's *Peer Gynt* suite.

Then, after ten minutes or so, a quartet of violinists straggled in from a music lesson, which had started during the lunch break, and had to be brought up to date on what the other children were doing. Some time later, when discussion had ended and the writing proper was under way, the general assistant came in with a bundle of school photographs to be given out at the end of the day. These caused a tremor of interest which had to be suppressed. A little later still, a boy crashed to the floor in a clatter of chair legs because he found it hard to think about monsters and not tilt his chair back at the same time. I paced steadily round the classroom, looking over shoulders, wishing that I'd made more time to read poems to the children, worrying at the slow progress of some and the heavy sighs of others. The children were, on the whole, quiet and they did their best but it was industry I sensed in the atmosphere rather than inspiration, duty rather than intent.

By considering the lesson and the poems it produced, it should be possible to come to some conclusions about what needs correcting in the way these lessons are conducted.

(a)   It wasn't sufficiently clear to the children what I meant when I asked them to write a poem. Some of them thought of poetry in a very restricted way.

(b)   I did not show enough enthusiasm for poetry and writing. I assumed that if the activity had any value and potential for enjoyment those things in themselves would get through to the children. I should, however, have made more efforts to 'sell' poetry.

(c) In spite of my interest in poetry and writing, I was the only member of the class not writing. What did this make the children think about the task? That, when you become old enough and have passed through the educational system, you are allowed to drop writing? That it has no relevance in the 'outside world'?

(d) I wasn't sure why we were writing. Did the children know why they were writing? Were they writing to please me? To turn in a piece of work that was correct in the way that a sum can be correct? To create a poem good enough to go on the wall or to be read out in assembly? Or for some other reason?

(e) I thought of the children as pupils rather than poets. I did not expect them to write freely, giving expression to their own thoughts and feelings. I hoped that they would come up with something that looked like a poem, that demonstrated that they were 'getting on all right' at school.

(f) The children were trying to write my poem rather than their own. The idea for it came from my planning and the stimulus provided by me.

(g) The subject that I set for writing was itself too restricted. It didn't allow the children room to manoeuvre. They were not able to follow up their own ideas about monsters in their own way because I had prepared the ground in the wrong manner. I talked them into providing descriptions of monsters when some of them may have wanted to write about other things.

(h) The atmosphere was not as conducive to writing as it might have been. I could have avoided the late arrival of the violinists and put off the appearance of the school photographs. (I could even have anticipated the boy's crash to the floor. Since I knew he had a tendency to collapse in this way, I could have started with him on the floor.)

(i) The children didn't have enough time for writing. They certainly didn't have enough time for thinking. On the other hand, they were helped by their familiarity with the subject. Encountering the Minotaur, Medusa and others through our work on Greek myths provided them with some pre-writing thinking time but they didn't have enough time to bring a poem from the conception of the first idea to the final writing out. It was not fair to expect them to do so.

(j) The poems the children wrote were first drafts. I am never content with the first draft of anything I write. It is not reasonable of me to expect the children to turn in finished poems in a single draft.

(k) I hadn't prepared them well enough to cope with some of the technical problems of writing. Their rhyming, for example, tended to be crude. Few of the children showed much awareness of rhythm. Just as I had over-prepared the subject for writing, I had under-prepared the means for tackling it.

(l)   I was too concerned about neatness, correctness and the presentation of what was being written.

(m)   I had no strategies for those who were stumped. Children who could find no way into the subject had to struggle to put something on paper and abandon hope of it being original or lively.

(n)   Having coaxed the children into writing with all these drawbacks and obstacles in the way, I hardly knew how to respond to their efforts. To comment on their creativity seemed impertinent. To correct their English seemed a pedantic and frustrating thing to do, like judging a choir on the straightness of its lines and the whiteness of its shirts.

It isn't easy to set right all that is wrong here. While some faults can be corrected quickly, others require a fundamental shift in attitude and approach which will take time. The chapters which follow attempt to show how one can move from the piecemeal and unsatisfactory method described above towards one which has more integrity and is more genuinely rewarding.

2 What is poetry?

A definition

Poetry is playing with language and images.

The word 'play' is important here. Playing with language can mean relishing sounds or rhythms. It also implies enjoyment, experiment, risk. At the same time, it does not deny the possibility of seriousness. Some games need to be played seriously in order to be enjoyed properly.

The purpose of this play is to say something about ourselves and our relationship to the world. What is said need not be portentous. If we laugh at what we see we are still saying something about the world and ourselves.

Poetry should produce an effect in those who read or hear it.

Gwendolen Fairfax, in *The Importance of Being Earnest*, recoils from the prospect of marrying someone with the name of John. 'It does not thrill', she says, 'It produces absolutely *no* vibrations.' What did thrill and produce vibrations in Gwendolen was, innocently enough, the name Ernest. Whilst this can hardly stand by itself as a poem, it seems to do for Gwendolen what poetry should do for its readers and hearers. Whether a poem thrills or not is, to a large extent, a subjective matter. For example, I find the following, from *Troilus and Cressida*, thrilling in its way:

> Time hath, my lord, a wallet at his back
> Wherein he puts alms for oblivion,
> A great-siz'd monster of ingratitudes.
>
> *William Shakespeare*

I can quite understand how the same lines could have the effect on someone else that the name John had on Gwendolen Fairfax. What I cannot fully understand is how those lines have an effect on me. I seemed to respond to them before I had fathomed what they were about.

Perhaps this aspect of poetry – its ability to thrill in this peculiar way – is the most important part of any definition. If you can find what is thrilling to you and to your class, and if you can make it sound thrilling, a lot of the teaching of poetry will already be done.

Why bother with a definition of poetry?

It is, I suppose, quite likely that you have thought of examples that fail to meet the requirements of the definition I've just given, and yet are undoubtedly poems. Poetry is, indeed, notoriously resistant to definition. A balance has to be struck between saying something so complex and detailed that it is difficult to grasp (and therefore not very useful), and saying something so simple and bland that it amounts to almost nothing.

It could be argued that, if poems form a natural part of our class routine, a definition of poetry already exists: an *unspoken* definition. When we tell children we are going to read them a poem, they know more or less what to expect. Have they not learned what poetry is from the way that poetry is used? Is it really necessary to make this definition explicit? Isn't it a waste of time to think about such abstract matters when the children are so obviously unconcerned about them? We all know what we're talking about (someone in the staffroom is bound to say) so why don't we just get on with it?

A teacher's inner debate about what poetry is (or his debate with colleagues, if he's lucky) will certainly be worthwhile and should improve his teaching. This is so whether he reaches a fixed and satisfying definition or not. If he doesn't even make the attempt, his thinking is likely to become stuck in an unimaginative and unquestioning rut. He will miss opportunities. As a consequence, his children's writing may become flat and stale, merely imitative of what they think poetry should be, of the unspoken definition.

This is why so many children, when they are asked to write 'a poem', set down banal ideas which they force into inept rhymes and decorate with coloured margins. What they produce is often a well-meaning attempt at what they think their teacher thinks is a poem. However, if their teacher is continually reviewing his own notions about poetry, their attempts at writing are likely to be fresher and more challenging.

Indeed, a lot of teaching comes to life when teachers, through questioning and debate, claim the subjects that they teach as their own. They teach best when they don't accept the unspoken definition of poetry (or games, or drama, or whatever) and, instead, forge a definition that has a particular meaning for them. Teaching poetry is most exciting and purposeful when you are teaching poetry as *you* understand it.

Children's first encounters with poetry are often accompanied by an instinctive joy and understanding which we, as adults, miss. Instead, we have to attempt a constant re-examination of what poetry is and how it works, 'a new shuffle of cards behind the brain' (Louis MacNeice).

Therefore let my definition stand as the opening remarks in a debate, nothing more, and let us take a closer look at the elements that make it up. These are, chiefly, language and images.

Poetry and language

Sometimes poetry is an attempt to make language very precise, sometimes it plays jokes with it, and sometimes it makes music with it. Poetry does not simply require language to get its message across. There is more to it than that. Every poem is, to a greater or lesser extent, about both its chosen subject *and* the language it uses to celebrate that subject. Poetry exhibits this strong link between sound and subject matter more consistently than any other form of writing. When the marriage of word and meaning is so secure that one cannot be altered without damage to the other, poetry is at its most powerful.

This is nothing to do with fine-sounding words as such. It is to do with *aptness* and may be expressed in the most straightforward language. When we ask children to write we should help them to focus their attention on what they mean and how their words sound. It should become apparent to them that words have a special impact and cannot always be put down at random and in any order.

Poetry and images

In poetry, images are set up or juxtaposed in odd and challenging ways that make us take a closer look at the world. They make us look again at the world we thought we knew, or beyond it to a world we might otherwise not notice at all.

Lorenzo in *The Merchant of Venice* says:

How sweet the moonlight sleeps upon this bank!

He sets up the strange notion that moonlight is something which *can* sleep. The unexpectedness of this idea helps us to form a clear picture of the bank of which he speaks. Wilfred Owen does a similar thing in his poem 'Futility' about a dead soldier:

Move him into the sun –
Gently its touch awoke him once

Here the sun can wake a person as a parent might wake a child. In the world which Owen and Shakespeare show us through these lines, the sun and the moon do more than light our way. They throw a particular, significant light on the world. It doesn't mean that we have to deny scientific evidence about the sun and the moon and accept them as powerful, personal deities instead. What it means is that there is a world beyond the immediately observable, beyond the bare facts we gather through our senses. A world in which the moon can sleep, or the sun wake sleepers, can help us make sense of our lives, and is often the special realm of poetry.

Theseus, in *A Midsummer Night's Dream*, says:

> The poet's eye, in a fine frenzy rolling,
> Doth glance from heaven to earth, from earth to heaven;
> And as imagination bodies forth
> The forms of things unknown, the poet's pen
> Turns them to shapes, and gives to airy nothing
> A local habitation and a name.
>
> > *William Shakespeare*

Siegfried Sassoon's poem 'A Footnote on the War' tells of a man who kept a diary of his experiences during the First World War. The poem is sad because the man knows that, for all its gravity, the diary fails to record what the war was really like. The diarist lacks what Sassoon calls the 'craft to snare the authentic moments of reality.' That is what poetry is specially good at: snaring authentic moments of reality. The moments must be real, of course. They must be real for the children and not imposed by a teacher.

Beyond a definition

It is important to make one's definition of poetry broad enough to include examples from sources beyond the conventional poetry anthologies. (That's why I made my definition of poetry so brief and spare: I wanted it to encompass many forms of expression.) Children's experience, as well as their ability to write, can be expanded by having their attention drawn to words and ideas that look interesting on the page or sound interesting when heard, whether they are classified as poems or not. The relationship between jokes and language, for example, is a crucial one. It matters *how* jokes are told, and certain words, as well as certain rhythms, are vital to the success of jokes.

By attending to the whole range of written or spoken communication, children can develop a poet's eye for an idea and a poet's ear for language. As teachers, we will be helped by a willingness to blur the boundaries between poetry and other forms in which language is used. We can find examples of – and inspiration for – poetic writing by blurring the boundaries between poetry and drama, stories, prose and speech.

Drama

Under Milk Wood is a play for voices. Bits of it are obviously 'poetic', obviously intended to be verse. Other bits, however, seem to be just as obviously ordinary speech. The neighbours who delight in discussing the awful and engaging Mr Waldo speak of him as follows:

> Black as a chimbley ...
> Ringing doorbells ...
> Making mudpies ...

Stealing currants . . .
Chalking words . . .
Saw him in the bushes . . .
Playing mwchins . . .
Send him to bed without any supper . . .
Give him sennapods and lock him in the dark . . .
Off to the reformatory . . .
Off to the reformatory . . .
Learn him with a slipper on his b.t.m.

Dylan Thomas

This employs a wonderfully lively vocabulary, has a definite rhythm and a poetic shape. Is it poetry? Is it intended to be poetry? The fact that it is so difficult to pin down makes no difference to its impact in the play. *Under Milk Wood* almost always 'works' and, like all good plays, takes language and uses it in a powerful way to make its point. Some of it is accessible to children and can be used to show them how fascinating language can be. Because *Under Milk Wood* is half way to poetry already it makes a good example, providing lots of instances of words and phrases which have dramatic impact. Other plays within the reach and experience of children will do the same kind of thing though.

Advertisements, television dramas, pantomimes, etc. are worth listening to for the language in which they are couched. Sometimes that language is wooden, flat, crude, imprecise or indistinct. It *can*, however, be immediate, vigorous or powerful, and language like that is the stuff of poetry.

Stories

Well-written stories also pay a great deal of attention to language. Some of them contain passages that stay in the mind and reverberate in the way that poetry does. Here is the opening of William Mayne's *The Jersey Shore*:

> The morning landscape was the same. Arthur himself felt he had been slept in, the train felt as if it had been slept in, and the country outside seemed to have stood still all night.

This could be written as a poem, not because it uses conventional and obvious 'poetic' words but because the ideas are interesting in a poetic way. They touch on that slightly odd world just beyond our normal experience. They sound good and can be arranged to break into lines:

> The morning landscape was the same.
> Arthur himself felt he had been slept in,
> The train felt as if it had been slept in,
> And the country outside seemed to have
> Stood still
> All night.

I took two lines to write the last four words because they seemed to me to demand it; they seemed to require two lines so that the great length of a night travelling on a train comes over more clearly. You might arrange it another way.

Of course, this is taking a liberty with Mayne's prose in order to make a point. If Mayne had intended to write verse, no doubt that's what he would have done. However, an activity like this can help us to see things with a poet's eye. We can try things out with a poet's ear and discover that poetry, or something a lot like it, can be found outside what we usually call poems.

This can be a useful exercise for children to try. Some passage from a story that appeals to them can be examined for its poetic potential. The opening of a book is a good place to start since authors tend to be very careful about openings. The advantage of an exercise like this is that children can concentrate on some of the important aspects of poetry without having to provide the original idea or find their own language. What they are likely to end up with is a *joint* poem, inspired by the original author and interpreted through their own insights about the passage.

If this seems a fairly sophisticated activity, it might be undertaken in a small group so that questions of line endings, words which might be omitted, words or phrases which might be repeated or rearranged, can be discussed.

Other prose

Some very unlikely sources can offer an opportunity for trying out poetic sensibilities. All that is required is an alertness to what may have the ring of a poem about it. Alan Brownjohn's 'Common Sense' is a good example. In this poem Brownjohn has used the words of an old school textbook and taken the title of the book as the refrain:

> An agricultural labourer, who has
> A wife and four children, receives 20s a week.
> $\frac{3}{4}$ buys food, and the members of the family
> Have three meals a day.
> How much is that per person per meal?
> – From *Pitman's Common Sense Arithmetic*, 1917

> A gardener, paid 24s a week, is
> Fined $\frac{1}{3}$ if he comes to work late.
> At the end of 26 weeks, he receives
> £30/5s/3d. How
> Often was he late?
> – From *Pitman's Common Sense Arithmetic*, 1917

The words are as they appear in the original textbook. What Brownjohn has done is focus on them in a special way and point out what they are saying about the way people used to live and regard each other in 1917. It ends:

Out of an army of 28,000 men,
15% were
Killed, 25% were
Wounded. Calculate
How many men there were left to fight.
    – From Pitman's Common Sense Arithmetic, 1917

These sums are offered to
That host of young people in our Elementary Schools, who
Are so ardently desirous of setting
Foot upon the first rung of the
Educational ladder ...
    – From Pitman's Common Sense Arithmetic, 1917

Speech

One of the most fertile grounds for discovering richness in language and strangeness of ideas is the speech we hear around us every day. Snatches of conversation overheard in shops can become the starting point for speculation which may lead to a poem. The speech which people use when they are unguarded, when they are not being particularly careful about their audience, has a life and an immediacy which defies capture by considered and 'correct' English. When we are swept along by what we have to say, in telling a story or in making a point, we often stumble across extremely vivid forms of expression. Poets like Auden, Frost and Larkin make excellent use of ordinary speech in their verse. Frost's poem 'A Time to Talk' is an example of verse expressed in simple language and with the rhythms of ordinary speech:

When a friend calls to me from the road
And slows his horse to a meaning walk,
I don't stand still and look around
On all the hills I haven't hoed,
And shout from where I am, 'What is it?'
No, not as there is a time to talk.
I thrust my hoe in the mellow ground,
Blade-end up and five feet tall,
And plod: I go up to the stone wall
For a friendly visit.

    Robert Frost

Finding poetry in prose, drama, stories and speech helps to enrich children's writing. Sometimes it is a good idea to ask the children simply to write; not to write a 'poem', or a 'story', or 'dialogue', but just to write and see what form the writing takes. Sometimes the writing will stay relentlessly in prose or will drift into the kind of narrative that will become a story. Sometimes it will begin to look like a poem. A good teacher can help a child see which way her writing is going. If the writing seems to stick between, say, poetry and drama, does it matter? Is it not better to be able to say that a piece of writing is sensitive and true than to fix it with the label 'poem' or 'play' or 'story'?

Poem or exercise?

Two children sit down to write. Each produces a piece of work which, for the moment, we will call a poem. The quality of their writing appears to be similar: there is nothing in particular to distinguish one piece from the other. However, although one child has been properly engaged in writing a poem, the other has been doing an exercise. One child has been prompted from within to write about things that matter to her while the other has responded dutifully to the instructions of her teacher.

By 'exercise' I do not mean the obvious textbook exercise which sets out a number of questions and tasks – answer the questions and you'll end up with a poem. The sort of exercise I am referring to is more subtle than that. It provides the children with the *elements* of a poem, sometimes with strategies for assembling the elements, and invites them to put these elements together. The assembled elements are then called a poem. For example, children are sometimes asked for words and phrases which are collected together, written up on the board and then used in thirty different versions of the same poem. What this produces is, in a sense, a bit like a poem. But it is far more like an exercise.

It is probably putting things too strongly to say that the difference between what our two children are doing is like the difference between someone making a picture and someone doing a jig-saw, but it is something like that. Poetry writing 'exercises' are not without value (see chapter 7). They often result in good, presentable work, and they give children valuable experience in language games and vocabulary building.

Of course, the situation we find in the classroom is not as simple as a choice between two extremes: shall we write a poem or shall we do an exercise? It is possible for the child who has been set the exercise to produce a piece of work which is more accessible and articulate than that produced by the child who is stirred to write from 'within'. Similarly, the child who has been set the exercise may, nevertheless, turn out a true poem while the child who has been encouraged to write with real feeling may produce something that resembles an exercise in its lifelessness. The heart of this matter is to be found in the reasons which lie behind our invitations to children to write.

We can ask children to write with the aim of producing pieces of work which can be attractively displayed. While there is nothing wrong with display as such (indeed, a poem displayed can boost a child's confidence), poems should not be written with display as the ultimate objective. Those pieces of work which are deemed not good enough for display, which are not 'presentable', come to be considered as failures. We may never mention the word failure, we may deliberately avoid it, but the child whose work is not displayed, when display is the be-all and end-all, may nevertheless regard herself as falling short of some objective and set standard. Poetry writing, she may conclude, is not something she does well. The solution is not to display everything regardless but to write for reasons which go beyond the production of display-board fodder.

There are other, clearer and more valuable reasons we can accommodate in our writing lessons:

- a concern for the way language is used
- a desire to get to the truth
- an effort to entertain
- an effort to understand

A concern for language

T. S. Eliot, in a famous passage from 'East Coker', talks about 'trying to learn to use words' and says that:

> ...every attempt
> Is a wholly new start, and a different kind of failure
> Because one has only learned to get the better of words
> For the thing one no longer has to say, or the way in which
> One is no longer disposed to say it. And so each venture
> Is a new beginning, a raid on the inarticulate
> With shabby equipment always deteriorating
> In the general mess of imprecision of feeling,
> Undisciplined squads of emotion.

When children write poetry they, as much as Eliot, should try to be precise and accurate. I have already said that poetry is both about its chosen subject and the language it uses to celebrate that subject. In teaching poetry we need to see that children look for the exact rather than the approximate word, the balanced rather than the clumsy phrase.

If this is one of our aims for writing, words and phrases which are rejected in the writing process need not be seen as failures. In writing about a dog, for example, we may put the word 'frisky' and then consider that it doesn't quite do what we want it to. The thinking that has accompanied our rejection of the word has been an important part of our creative activity.

Expressing the truth

Once children know what they want to say, they must say it as straightforwardly as they can, making the best use of the language they have available to them. This, of course, presupposes that they know what to say, and knowing what to say is the all-important first stage which precedes the word gathering. It is easy to forget this. It is easy to take a subject like 'an old man' and gather a collection of 'old man' words before assembling them into a poem. By doing this we may concentrate too much on the effects our chosen words create and not enough on what we actually want to say. It could be, for example, that we want to write about our *feelings* when we visit the old man who lives across the street. If we don't give proper attention to this impulse and, instead, forge ahead with our collection of 'old man' words, we may find ourselves writing the wrong poem and missing the truth we wanted to tell.

The truth need not be on a grand scale. We need not deal with the fundamental truths of human existence – life, love and death. To say exactly how a baby moves its fingers is also to tell a truth.

Poetry as entertainment

Humorous verse is often a good introduction to poetry for children. It is usually easier to understand than most other types of poetry, and there is something very attractive about playing with words and rhythms that seems to appeal to children. 'The Modern Hiawatha', for example, amuses by the lengths it goes to explain something quite simple, and by playing with the insistent rhythms of Longfellow's original:

> When he killed the Mudjokivis,
> Of the skin he made him mittens,
> Made them with the fur side inside,
> Made them with the skin side outside,
> He, to get the warm side inside,
> Put the inside skin side outside;
> He, to get the cold side outside,
> Put the warm side fur side inside.
> That's why he put fur side inside,
> Why he put the skin side outside,
> Why he turned them inside outside.
>
> George A. Strong

Poetry need not be solemn. At the same time, humorous poetry can still deal with the truth. 'Humour' said the American writer E. B. White, 'plays close to the big, hot fire which is truth and the reader often feels the heat.'

It is not always wise to ask children to *write* humorous verse – the results can be dire – but it is a good idea to remind them from time to time that poetry can be lighthearted.

Poetry as an aid to understanding

What a poet does not require is a thoroughgoing understanding of the subject she has chosen for her poem. In fact, the desire to understand, rather than the understanding itself, can prove a great spur to writing. The writing of a poem can help us to understand or at least come to terms with something that puzzles or fascinates us. We learn, both about our chosen subject and ourselves, in our efforts to be precise, to look beyond the obvious, to explore related images, to get our words on paper.

What we learn of ourselves is two-fold. We learn about ourselves in relation to the subject we are dealing with; and we learn about ourselves through the struggle to get the right words in the right order. Of course, few children will finish a piece of writing and be able to say 'Well, I feel I know myself much better for that experience.' The effects of writing true poetry are more subtle than that. They are, nevertheless, real.

We have seen that poetry is a matter of words – 'the best words in the best order', as Coleridge said – and of having something to say. It concerns not only an ability to use language accurately and purposefully, but also the engagement of feelings.

When we set about poetry writing with children we need to ask ourselves a vital question: do we want to produce poems or poets? Of course, if we *are* able to produce poets, they in their turn will produce the poems. However, it is easy to be satisfied with poems which impress parents or professional colleagues, and to pay comparatively little attention to whether the children who write them have been educated to see, hear and speak as poets.

3   The writing process

An actress preparing to play a part will go through a number of set actions – rituals almost – in order to feel right before she goes on stage. She may find it helpful to become still and silent and concentrate on her breathing. On the other hand she may need to become animated and chatter incessantly while she puts her dressing table in meticulous order. The same sort of thing is true of the batsman who is about to play an innings. Certain little things have to be done, and done in the same way and in the same order, before the innings proper can begin. Always put your cap on last. Swing your arms as you walk to the wicket. Try to see a bird in flight before you take guard. Or make sure you never see a bird in flight before you take guard. It really doesn't matter, as long as what you do helps you feel right.

This sort of preparation, odd and neurotic as it may sound, is more often than not a vital part of the writing process as well. It isn't simply that writers tend to be peculiar people who are pointlessly fussy about the way they write. They know that, unless conditions are right, they will be unable to say what they have to say as effectively as they should. Thus they must work at a desk where everything is in its precise and proper place, or at a desk which has been allowed to pile up with clutter and must not be touched. They must do their best work in the morning when the mind is fresh and active. Or they must work at night when imagination may creep up and take them by surprise. And so on.

Making sure that the conditions for work are right is only partly a matter of feeling psychologically up to the task. It is also very much concerned with practicalities. The batsman who swings his arms as he walks to the wicket is not only settling his mind, he is also loosening tense muscles. The actress who tidies her dressing table before playing a part is heightening her concentration as well as soothing her nerves.

If we ask children to write – and take their efforts seriously – we should be sensitive to the need for proper preparation and the right conditions. We should see that they are psychologically and practically ready to write. It is, after all, only fair. Professional writers go to great lengths to see that things are just so before they commit themselves to paper. If we expect children to commit themselves to paper we should try to provide them with conditions that are as propitious as possible.

What we need to do now is to look at the ways in which we might create these sorts of conditions. Firstly, we need to consider the *internal* conditions necessary for the writing process. This means not just psychological readiness – or mood, to put it more simply – but those things a child should store up within her in order to write well: things like self-discipline, self-confidence and openness to ideas. Secondly, we need to provide, to the best of our ability, the right sort of *external* conditions to ease the paths of the young writers we seek to encourage. How can we create an environment in time and space in which writing will flow, rather than one in which it is always being interrupted or stifled?

Internal Conditions

Mood

The time-honoured way of creating the mood for writing of any kind is to clap one's hands and bark, 'Right! Settle down!'

This is, perhaps, an instinctive acknowledgement that some sort of preparation is needed but there are subtler and ultimately more effective approaches. Of course, it isn't possible to set out all the routines and rituals which children might adopt so that they feel right for writing. Children, like all writers, are frustratingly individual. What settles one may irritate another. If you make them all stand on one leg and hum for three minutes you may, by chance, hit upon just the thing to increase the enthusiasm and fluency of some children. You are more likely, however, to achieve nothing. It is the children who are best suited to find out, through experiment, what is most likely to put them in the mood to write. The teacher's role is to encourage the search. He can, of course, *suggest* ways of preparing. Methods based on silence and concentration are most likely to be effective. But he can also be tolerant of genuine attempts by children to experiment.

To be realistic, it is unlikely that all your children will arrive at an exact set of circumstances designed to produce their best writing. After all, schools are not always the most conducive of surroundings. The sound of distant PE lessons, the smell of distant boiled cabbage can be distracting. However, it is possible to do *something* to prepare children before they start writing. You may choose to draw the line at the child who claims she can only write well in chalk on cardboard whilst sitting in the leafy seclusion of the big tree at the top of the school field. On the other hand, your acceptance of children who write best sitting on the floor rather than a chair (or whatever it is that they come up with) can improve the standard of genuine writing in your class. Deciding between proper experiment and a child's natural tendency to do something a bit daft is, like so much else in teaching, a matter of shrewd and careful judgement.

The advantage of making children aware of the need to prepare for writing is not simply that they may discover for themselves a formula for getting under way. It also puts a stronger emphasis on the *importance* of writing poetry. It helps them to take themselves seriously as writers and shows them that poetry is something for which you prepare as you may prepare to act a part or play in an important game. You don't just sit down and get on with it.

Lack of mood

What can you do when you don't feel like writing, when the muse refuses to come fluttering down to perch on your shoulder? The simple answer is that if you are not inspired then you must start writing without inspiration. You must do something. Make a note of random thoughts. Write down what it is that makes writing hard: 'I can't write about dogs because I don't like dogs.' Your negative feelings may be the key to a piece of writing you do want to undertake: 'What I don't like about dogs – a poem'. Sometimes it is possible to beat this blockage by freeing the mind from the intended subject and letting it take off in a completely different direction. A teacher should be prepared to allow this to happen.

Children can be shown that writing is sometimes difficult. It is my own experience that ideas sometimes flow so fast that I can hardly write quickly enough to keep up with them. On other occasions I have to wring an idea as hard as I can in order to extract a few drops of life-blood. I can't be sure until much later which piece of writing yields the best results, the easy piece or the hard piece.

I realise that there seems to be a contradiction here. I've just said that, when things are tough, you sit down and write anyway. Earlier I said that you don't simply sit down and get on with writing, you prepare. Both statements are true, I think. You don't just sit down and write, you prepare. If you've prepared and you don't feel like writing, then you just sit down and write. Sometimes the physical act of writing produces ideas where mere meditation produces nothing. It is as if ideas are only released when pen or pencil is in contact with paper, completing some sort of circuit. This is not a rule of thumb. Sometimes, usually when the ideas are flowing, it is a good idea to sit and think.

Self-discipline

How to tackle an absence of inspiration leads us on to an even more important aspect of the writing process: discipline. The fact that a writer must be disciplined does not mean that she must shut her mind to teeming fantasy and restrict herself to straight up-and-down fact and observation. It means she should develop good habits, those habits which enable her to express her vivid imaginings when they come to her.

The most important habit to acquire is that of editing your own work (see chapter 9). There is an idea, fairly prevalent if not actually expressed in schools, that poetry is oddly phrased language overlaid with adjectives and adjectival phrases which often rhyme. When you write a poem you switch your mind onto this adjectival track and your thoughts rattle along the line to end up as complete poems. This is, quite simply, false. In fact it is the sort of idea which is likely to clog children's thinking when they set about writing. By writing poems in drafts and then editing them children can write clearer, more precise and more effective work. Choose the simplest form of expression, question the words you have chosen, make a second draft, a third, as many as it takes. Try to be straightforward not colourful. If these habits are introduced as an accepted part of class procedure they will not appear tedious but as the best way to make sure you say what you mean.

To complicate the matter slightly, however, it should be remembered that sometimes a writer's first and hurried jottings on a subject hit the nail on the head. In fact, this is often the case with younger children for whom freshness can become lost through a lengthy editing process.

One of the most important things the more experienced writer must learn to do is *recognise* when a piece of work is 'right' and then leave it alone. A sensitive teacher can help a child with this problem. He can either say, 'Stop there! Any more fiddling and you'll spoil it', or he can encourage the poet to revise, trim, reshape and make another draft. There's no golden rule about which course to take, and mistakes are easy to make, but a teacher should be aware of the options. (Needless to say, he should refrain from suggesting his own 'good bits' to improve someone else's poem.)

Self-criticism and self-confidence

In order to develop self-discipline about writing a child should be sufficiently confident to be her own critic. This highlights another difficult role for the teacher. There must be a balance between self-criticism and self-confidence. What should be discouraged is the sort of criticism that inhibits any kind of creative act: 'I can't do that, I'm not good enough.' On the other hand we don't want children to assume that the work they submit is the best they can do. It may be but they shouldn't take it for granted.

One way a teacher can strike the right balance is to regard himself as the children's literary agent. Soothe them when they are afraid to start writing. Prod them when they are unnecessarily delaying. Praise and encourage them when they are on their way. Cosset them, protect them from knocks, convince them that what they have to say is unique, discourage complacence. All the time, as agent, you are trying to get your poets' best work to land on your desk so that you can do something with it (see chapter 10).

Self-expression

It is worth noting that the best writing is not always, and perhaps not often, an exploration of the self. Rather it is a looking-outward at the world. There is a temptation in schools to regard creative writing and self-expression as more or less the same thing. Self-expression is only a part of creative writing. It is true that strong feelings make good subjects for poems in schools, but too often we see the child entering her own poem to tell us how she feels when she would express herself better at a distance. The important distinction to be made here is that, while a poet should always feel strongly about her subject, that subject should not always be her strong feelings. It may help a child to write better if her teacher suggests writing poems without 'I' in them.

These remarks, and those on self-criticism and self-expression, apply largely to older children – those, say, of nine and upwards. With younger children, and those whose grasp of written language is immature, it is not advisable to hurry these stages. Editing should be introduced gradually. Children whose writing skills are comparatively raw should be encouraged to put down ideas as they come. Any attempt at serious editing at this stage is likely to discourage. In time, after a number of these 'one-draft' poems have been successfully written, the children can be asked to have a second look at their work. By the time they are capable of writing with some fluency they should also be familiar with the editing and drafting process (see chapter 9).

The same applies to the use of 'I' in poems. It is perfectly natural for young children to put themselves in their writing in this way, and they should be allowed to do so before the teacher suggests that they might try to write more objectively. There is no point in being dogmatic about what the children should be writing and it would be a mistake to stop them writing 'I' before they are ready.

Openness

Children can be encouraged to keep their ears and minds open for ideas from all sorts of sources. It sometimes happens that an image or a word occurs, out of a dream or a day-dream or apparently nothing, and is rejected because it seems strange or doesn't quite make sense. These words and images can often provide a poem with its most fascinating life. It doesn't matter if the full meaning of a poem hasn't been grasped by the poet. E. M. Forster has this to say on the subject:

> What about the creative state? In it a man is taken out of himself. He lets down as it were a bucket into his subconscious, and draws up something which is normally beyond his reach. He mixes this thing with his normal experiences, and out of the mixture he makes a work of art ... Such seems to be the creative process. It may employ much technical ingenuity and worldly knowledge, it may profit by critical standards, but mixed up with it is this stuff from the bucket, this subconscious stuff, which is not procurable on demand. And when the process is over ... the artist, looking back on it, will wonder how on earth he did it. And indeed he did not do it on earth.

This strange element of creativity is not, as Forster says, procurable on demand. You can't make it happen but you can make yourself open to its influence. The following poem, written by a child, illustrates this point well:

The Power of Imagination

A source coming from nowhere
Clears my mind from all other but it.
A reflection of a thought hidden in my mind.
I had not seen a human.
It had come and gone – not telling me
From where it came.
Yet my own thoughts destroyed it.
I have realised
Now
That it was nearly human –
It had nearly escaped from my imagination
But I rubbed it from my mind.
It no longer existed.

Joshua Holmes 9

A great many writers never go anywhere without a notebook in which to jot down quick observations, snatches of conversation or sudden ideas. For most children, perhaps, this is too sophisticated and ponderous an approach to writing poetry. Some, however, might welcome the suggestion. Writing is a continuous process of developing and shuffling ideas. I often find that some of my most satisfying writing takes place when I have been forced to abandon the typewriter and set off on the short walk to my place of work. Sometimes, indeed, I deliberately prolong a walk in order to let an idea work itself out as I go.

External conditions

Tools

Some writers I have spoken to feel they must write in pencil because to them a pencil is more immediate and in touch with what is going on in the writer's mind than any pen or typewriter. With pen or typewriter they feel distanced from what they want to say. Personally, I write a lot directly onto a typewriter because, in spite of its clatter and my hesitant typing, my writing works better that way. (I think it's something to do with the fact that I think at about the same pace at which I type: fairly slowly.)

Within reasonable bounds children should be encouraged to work with the materials which suit them best. The same applies to the size and neatness of the writing and to the spelling. As most of the time the children will be writing drafts of poems – even if there is little change between the first draft and the final copy – it hardly matters what the first draft looks like as long as the writer can read it. This is not to say that children should be allowed to write how they like with any old pen or pencil. What they should do is to find for themselves the tools and materials which help them to write at their best.

Time

It should be obvious by now that children who are going to take to writing poetry in any serious fashion will need time to do so. There aren't many writers who can sit down 'cold' and start straight away. Most need to give some time to preparation, perhaps to read what they have already written, and to feel their way in.

Ideas for poems occur in time. Some can be taken while they're fresh but others need time to grow and develop, a period of gestation before they are quite ripe. The consequence of this for classroom organisation is that the teacher should be prepared to be flexible. For example, a subject for writing could be raised at the beginning of the week, or earlier, and then discussed, pondered, chewed over, allowed to rest for a while before the children actually set about it. Similarly, children can work at their own poems, at their own pace, throughout the term. A subject may emerge from a current preoccupation of a particular class, even a particular child. A project on journeys may have taken off, something in the news may have fired imaginations. Whatever the origins, something that has induced ideas to come out to play, and allowed them time for that play, can help to make sure that these ideas are properly developed. As long as the children are aware that a poem may need some crafting over a period of time, and that the time is available to them, it shouldn't be necessary to make complicated amendments to the timetable.

I don't want to suggest that sessions in which all the children are writing at the same time are a bad idea. They can create a degree of concentration and intensity which a child working on her own may find hard to match. It can also be fun to write to a deadline. If children are asked to produce a page or so of writing in a short time without much attention to structure or self-criticism, the results can sometimes be liberating and worthwhile.

Another aspect of poetry writing often overlooked is repetition. It's easy to feel that because we have 'done' a particular topic in creative writing then we needn't do it again. Time given to another go at an old idea, or a repeated try at a certain technique, will often bring about new, more competent and sometimes fresh poems.

Surroundings

The modern classroom is constantly changing its identity. At one moment it is a debating chamber, the next a reading room, the next an art studio and so on. When the children are engaged in writing poetry it will help them if the room becomes like Eli Jenkins' front parlour in *Under Milk Wood*, a poem room. This need not require major structural alterations: the most important consideration is that the door will not burst open to reveal messengers of all sizes with all manner of messages, none of which is usually very pressing. Perhaps you can put up a notice: 'Please Keep Out – Poets At Work'. The likelihood is that it will take quite a struggle to establish certain times during which you hope your room will not be violated. Coleridge was troubled by an interruption from a single visitor from Porlock, who managed to drive away the poem he was engaged upon ('Kubla Khan'). Classrooms can appear to be peopled by persons from Porlock.

Almost certainly the best atmosphere for the writing of poetry is a quiet one, and the quietest moments come when the writers are so intent on what they are doing that, ironically, they become unaware of extraneous noises. However, some teachers feel they are not earning their keep unless they are in at the kill as a poem is written. Thus they pace about in the silence intoning good advice, 'Don't forget those adjectives we talked about!', rather like the invigilator of an exam who suddenly announces with dramatic resonance, 'You have five minutes left.' Really a teacher should not seek to influence the writing of a poem in this way. Not only should he respect the silence, he should also respect the fact that what the children write is their own. His job is to encourage and advise but at the moment of creation he should make himself as unobtrusive as possible. Some children may need immediate assistance but this can be given with the minimum of fuss and distraction.

You may find that simply stating that writing is about to begin and putting up your 'Keep Out' sign is enough to make the room feel right for poetry. The children will, of course, add their own preparations to this, taking up their favourite positions, moving to a chosen corner, taking out their poetry pencils – whatever it is that makes them feel best prepared. You may, on the other hand, wish to make some subtle change to the look of the room. The drawing of blinds, the draping of a piece of material across the blackboard, the setting out of a particular vase – things like these may be incorporated as a class's private ritual to signify the start of something important – part fun and part a serious attempt to create mood.

Purpose

No one, child or adult, is going to feel inclined to write a piece to the very best of her ability if the piece is destined to become nothing more than marking fodder. There must be more to it than that. Children writing poetry are not simply engaging in curriculum activity – they are making something. Of course, it is always possible to make things for the joy of making them, but that's not quite the same as making them for the joy of having them corrected.

Children can write because they are compiling their own anthologies, or because they want to present their poem in an assembly or to a child in another class. They can write because they wish to contribute to a school magazine, to provide part of a script for a play or a slide and music presentation, or to contribute to a radio or television programme. They can, it goes without saying, write to express themselves. If they don't write for a real purpose their writing will lack an essential kick. The teacher should see that the purpose is clear from the start. It isn't really sufficient to decorate and double-mount a poem for some open evening. That's *retrospective* purpose and as such can't make any contribution to the writing process.

Because the writing process is such a difficult thing to pin down, and because it is different for every child who writes (it can even be different at different times for each individual), what I have had to say about it is full of contradictions: You must be disciplined, you must be free; you must allow time, you can write effectively to strict deadlines; you must edit, you can get sincerity and freshness from instant jottings. This, I'm afraid, is the nature of the beast. It won't submit itself to simple rules. It's a point we make more than once. Writing poetry is not necessarily easy and teaching it demands sensitivity, understanding and skill on the part of the teacher. These things don't come without a willingness to become involved and to invest time and effort.

The role of the teacher in preparing the external conditions for the writing process is comparatively straightforward. There are things that you can actually do to smooth the path, like providing materials and seeing that children aren't interrupted when they write. The teacher's role in helping children with the internal conditions for writing is, on the other hand, no easy matter. It is like much else that he has to do in the teaching day – subtle, demanding, full of pitfalls and very important.

'I am a poet!'

(Sophie Ladds thought up this slogan for a home-made badge)

4   Helping children begin writing poetry

In this chapter I intend to focus on ways we can help children to begin writing poetry. The suggestions here are geared to the first few times a teacher tackles poetry with his class. A vital preliminary is that the pupils have enjoyed having poetry read to them recently. Children will write better if they have a sense of what poetry does, and they will learn this by being immersed in poetry.

There is a widespread lack of interest, even hostility, towards poetry today, held by adults and children alike, in school as well as outside. It is commonplace to hear groans from pupils when the word poetry is mentioned. This reaction is mainly due to ignorance and will not last long if the teacher presents poetry in a positive way. But it is as well to circumvent a negative reaction by simply reading poetry to children without previously announcing the intention to do so. The student teacher who launches into a lively poem will receive a better response from his pupils than if he begins with, 'Now I am going to read you a few poems.' It takes children off their guard, before prejudice has a chance to creep in. Or hand round some inviting anthologies, asking each child to select a favourite poem to read to others in the group. And in the early writing sessions, a teacher can begin by introducing an interesting theme without making it explicit at first that poetry will be the end result. It won't be long before they are hooked. Many of your pupils will find that poetry is a more approachable form of writing than, say, narrative or report. Younger and less able pupils will be amazed at the relative ease of success in their writing. Most will find it a very satisfying mode of writing. Even the odd few (and in our experience it is only the odd few) who don't take to writing it are likely to discover some poets they enjoy reading.

Before I get down to specific examples, let me make a few points about beginning poetry with children. You can offer this advice before the writing starts.

1. **Poems do not have to rhyme**: in fact, it can be a good idea to ban rhyme initially. A very small number of children are natural rhymers, but they can explore this talent at a later stage. Most children find it difficult to concentrate on rhyme at first, and do so at the expense of everything else. Forced rhyme tends to lead to banal or 'silly' verse and certainly to the

absence of real meaning or feeling. (Though certain sorts of rhyme can be used to advantage in the early stages, see pages 47–50 and 80.) If you want children to write free verse, make sure you present them with plenty of examples of free verse or confusion is likely. I have known inexperienced student teachers read children three strongly rhythmic, rhyming poems and then ask for free verse.

2. **Take a new line when you pause**: pupils can be advised to write poetry by taking a new line at a natural pause. In the early sessions, I often race round the class actually putting the pupil's first few ideas down on paper for her, using only her own words, of course. Thus, in just a moment or two of individual attention, the pupil can see and hear what her poem looks and sounds like. Most children find this extremely motivating, whatever their age. A few do not care for such disturbance, and I quickly learn to leave them alone.

   The instructions are very simple. The teacher can introduce some topic of interest, get the children excited and talking, then suggest they write about the topic, taking a new line at each pause. It is as well not to worry about punctuation at this stage, unless the children are otherwise sophisticated writers. Naturally enough, not all children will manage even this simple shaping at first, but it is easy to help them. The child can be asked to read her work aloud, listening for pauses which the teacher transcribes into a poem. It is important that the pupil decides herself where the pauses come. After a couple of lines have been written in this way, many pupils can get on by themselves.

   Others may need more time spent on a one-to-one basis with the teacher. If they find the task very difficult, the teacher can re-read the child's writing, pausing at different places, letting the child choose which sounded best. The fact that the same words will sound different depending on where the pauses come (i.e. where the lines end) is interesting to most children who like this control over their own writing which can be so difficult to compose.

3. **Say something fresh**: I try to encourage each child to find the words that only *she* would use, to look at the subject in her own way and to find something new to say about it. I stress that we are not looking for something that is earth-shattering. Each individual has a unique 'voice', just as she has a unique face – it is a question of finding that personal 'voice' and having the confidence to use it. Poor writing is often a second rate attempt to mimic the writing of others. Most children's early attempts at poetry look rather ordinary and don't smack of the 'original', but if they are using their own words to express their own ideas, that is an excellent start.

4. **Ordinary things make good poetry**: the ordinary stuff of everyday life can be used to good effect for poetry. The world of fantasy and imagination can be exciting too, but most poetry begins with the individual perhaps

looking inside herself or outside at the world around.

5. **Poetry is the art of compression**: I explain this to children by stressing that every word in a poem should be there for a purpose, should add to the poem in some way. If it does not, it should be excluded. This quickly gets rid of unnecessary 'ands', 'thens' and even superfluous direct and indirect articles. Later it can lead to more sophisticated pruning. Children begin to see the point of the maxim that 'brevity is the soul of wit', and that poems have more bite when language is used in an economical way.

It depends on the age and experience of your pupils, how many of these guidelines are introduced at any given time. At a first session with six- to seven-year-olds, it might be enough to say that poems do not have to rhyme. In a one-off poetry workshop with adults, I might refer to all five points.

When the writing starts

At first it can be productive to spend a fair bit of time working co-operatively with a pupil. A few younger or less able pupils may need this individual attention until confidence is built up. Some pupils are able to cope with a teacher's written suggestions for shaping a poem by the use of strokes on the text. The first few lines can be indicated, then the pupil is expected to redraft the rest of the piece for herself. It is essential that, if this sort of help takes place, the pupil is aware that the teacher's shaping is one possibility out of many, and that there are alternatives she herself may prefer.

Many pupils begin writing poetry with a sort of descriptive prose. What follows is an example of what I call a piece of prose that 'wants to be a poem'. This eight-year-old was asked to write about fears at night. Cover up the rest of the page and concentrate on the writing. What do you think of it?

Now look at the same material shaped into a poem:

I wonder who could be behind me.
My mind went through many things.
I thought I heard an owl.
I looked behind.
The sky looked like a black blanket
    with silver in the sky.
The moon looked like silk in the silver.
The owl looked like it was in the moon.
The branches crackled
I jump.   I look ahead.
    The leaves rustle.
Shivers run down my back.
I get home.
        I am scared.

Anisa 8

How easy it is to overlook the quality of Anisa's writing by concentrating on surface features of language like handwriting, spelling and punctuation. In fact, it is a most successful 'poem' by a first year junior for whom English is a second language.

(I 'shaped' this poem in one out of many possible ways to show how I encourage children to begin experimenting with where the words go on the page.)

'Free verse'

It is easier to encourage our pupils to write simple free verse straight away. For some children this does require personal attention, often with the teacher as scribe for the child's initial ideas. The conversation might go something like this:

'I don't know what to write./ I don't know how to write it as a poem.'

'O.K. We are thinking about cats. Have you decided on a particular cat? Good, now fix that cat in your mind. Close your eyes and see him. Take a really close look at him. Where is he now? What is he doing? What sort of cat is he? You might like to begin your poem there with the cat in your head you've just looked at.'

(*Pause – the pupil needs a little time.*)

'Can you give me a first line and I'll write it down?/ What can you see?/ Tell me about the cat.'
'Well ... he's sitting on the rug in front of the fire licking his paws ...'

'Let's get that down. What exactly would you like me to write?'

Sitting on the rug in front of the fire

'What shall I say – the cat, our cat, his name?'

Our cat licks his paws.

'How does he lick his paws?/ What colour are his paws?/ Can you see his tongue?'

First the right one
Then the left.
He makes his gingery fur
all wet ...

'Let me read this back to you. It's a good start. Are you happy with it? Shall we go on? Do you want to say any more about the cat/the rug/the fire? Some more about the lazy cat in front of the fire? Or is he going to move and do something different?'

The skill lies in our questioning. A child who has begun a poem with flair may be satisfied with a general comment like: 'That's a lovely beginning. I'm looking forward to seeing the rest of it.' A child who begins laboriously may find specific questions useful to help her bring the poem to life.

Rhythm

What I have been discussing so far is a method for allowing children to tap, to become aware of the natural rhythms of language and to harness this for poetry by shaping it into lines. As I hope I have made clear, there are no absolutes here. We cannot tell our pupils where a line should end or another begin with any certainty. And we certainly want our pupils to make these decisions for themselves. One thing I am sure of is that the best poetry, as Robert Frost says, is where 'the feeling has found the form and the form has found the words.' The form of a poem (i.e. the poem shaped into lines) is inextricably bound up with its rhythm. I am referring in this instance to the natural rhythms of spoken language which can be captured in poetry, if we take a little time to listen to ourselves, and not to formal or regular metre imposed on writing. We all have an instinct for rhythm, but this is undoubtedly more developed in people who have experienced a great deal of poetry. (For a more detailed discussion of rhythm, see chapter 7.)

Finally in this section dealing with general points about starting poetry, I know of no better advice than that offered to young writers by Ted Hughes in *Poetry in the Making*:

Imagine what you are writing about – see it, live it, look at it, touch it, smell it, listen to it – turn yourself into it – then the words look after themselves – like magic.

Specific approaches for beginning poetry

Haiku poetry

Now for the first of specific ways of leading into writing with children – namely haiku-type poems. This is the most successful spring-board for poetry I have come across, and many dozens of teachers have agreed with this verdict. Haiku is a form of Japanese poetry which has been written for several hundred years. Traditionally it follows a three line, five-seven-five syllable format. Of course, young writers could not be expected to manage such a tight structure in their early attempts at poetry. So I ask the children to write haiku-type poems, three lines long, where the last line is shorter than the middle one. I do not bother about syllables at this stage.

Let's look at haiku a bit more closely by considering some examples by masters of this craft:

> On a bare branch
> a rook roosts
> autumn dusk.

Matsuo Basho

> The first cold showers pour
> Even the monkey seems to want
> a little coat of straw.

Matsuo Basho

> These morning airs –
> one can see them stirring
> caterpillar hairs.

Yosa Buson

> At the butterflies
> the caged bird gazes, envying –
> just watch its eyes.

Kobayashi Issa

(Notice the differing format and punctuation of these translations. Translations vary in quality. They also rarely retain the original syllable count.)

These poems aptly illustrate some of the conventions of haiku. Haiku contain a reference to a season. This may occur directly as in Basho's 'autumn dusk' or indirectly by allusion to the weather or some aspect of nature. Haiku evoke emotion: they deal with the sensitive, thoughtful moments in our lives, often through the power of suggestion. The mood of a poem may be triggered by use of contrast: the caged bird envying the freedom of the butterflies, the morning breeze which makes even the tiny caterpillar's hair billow. Haiku have been likened to Japanese ink sketches – a few strokes create a picture, a few words suggest a scene, experience, feeling. Clearly this is a very concentrated form of poetry, where the poet aims to capture the essence of an experience in everyday language. Despite their brevity and simplicity, haiku are often profound poems which act as a starting-point for a train of thought or emotion. They are representational – the common experience of mankind is evoked by looking closely at one small part of it, captured in only three lines.

Children tend to respond positively to haiku. They like poetry which is short, has immediate appeal and is uncomplicated. When I use haiku with children, I make sure they see as well as hear what they are like. If time permits, I set up a small Japanese display with pictures, lettering, porcelain and a miniature tree. This arouses initial interest. After reading several haiku, I discuss some of the features already mentioned. I often stress the miniature element in haiku: a few words can convey a great deal. I encourage the children to look at some aspect of the world with new eyes, as if they had never seen it before. My instructions might follow this sort of pattern:

• write a poem with only three lines
• take a new line when you come to a pause
• make the last line shorter than the middle one
• make every word count

With top juniors I might suggest that the second line runs into the third line or the first into the second, as in the examples above.

Titles that have worked well are: Night, Daybreak, Rain, Sadness, Anger, A Tree, Birds and Animals. Here are several haiku on Night written by first year juniors at a one-off poetry session with me:

> Shadows creeping across the wall.
> I sit up in bed
> too afraid to scream.
>
> *Anna 8*

> In the night I feel
> as if the wind is rocking the house
> from side to side.
>
> *Jonathan 8*

> In bed at night
> I hear the trees rustling
> like a plague of locusts.
>
> *Sean 8*

> Clatters on my window
> only rain
> Scarey
>
> *Satish 8*

Already these children are writing poems full of promise. The condensed language is there: allusions, comparisons, similes. And most importantly, these children were delighted with their first efforts at writing poetry and eager to try again.

Where do you go from here? In the next session you could try haiku again, using a different topic or offering the children their own choice of subject matter. You could help individuals with whatever weaknesses were evident in their work. Some children write very long lines and need to prune, some don't know where to end their lines, for others it is difficult not to write stories. If the children need a change (and some are not able to cope with reviewing and improving their work in this way at first), introduce a fresh theme, something very approachable like writing about an animal or some interesting object you've brought in. Ask the children to write a haiku-type poem again, but this time to add one or two extra lines. Soon most of them will be well on the way to writing simple free verse poems.

One reason why haiku works so well as a starting-point for poetry is that it is one of the furthest points in poetry from rhyme. Most children are convinced that poetry and rhyme are inextricably enmeshed. That is no surprise as so much verse for the young is in rhyme, and rhyme is extremely pleasurable and satisfying. But haiku offers a way into poetry which highlights imagery and effective language without focusing on rhyme. All children are capable of writing, or at least composing such poetry, even if it is dictated to the teacher who writes it down verbatim. It is a particularly useful device for young children. Cathy Pompe, a teacher colleague who was working with five-year-olds, describes her experience of haiku:

'The writing powers of infants lag disappointingly behind their thoughts. Writing a story, a child will start with a picture, vivid, alive, in his mind, the setting will unfold excitingly around him, and then the lack of writing skills makes the whole thing grow stale, the story peters out or comes to an abrupt end.

Poetry writing, especially haiku, is probably the most meaningful way of encapsulating thought, idea, feeling and image alive, and it is accessible to the poorest writer. Over a year it is possible to train a class to use language in a poetry specific way. It is a heightened experience, it's short and it's not stressful.

I accept their utterances as they stand. The child feels his unique thought bubble, taken intact, mattering. I tell the children a haiku is a small jewel, precious words condensed into the middle of the page. I tell them to leave out the boring words like "the", "and", "then", "is", etc. Talking to the class together, I will string together at random three of the best word clusters that have been thrown up by different children while we've been thinking. Maybe juggle the order to show there is no right or wrong and say, "See, that's beautiful, that's packed with ideas. That's all you need." In this way the writing is usually powerful, boiled down, nothing left but valuable words. Here are two such poems after visiting the Botanics on a crisp winter's day.'

Frosty day
Ice is sprinkling off the trees
and the trees are shining.

Susan 5

Today is frosty
all white
like icing on the cake.

Jack 5

Let's close this section with a few examples of haiku written by children of various ages in early attempts at poetry. I am sure you will agree that these children have travelled a fair distance on the road to writing successful poetry.

Night
Black faces with eyes looking in them
Twinkling in the black night.
Shadows hiding.

Ross 6

Dark when the creaks all come.
I might have heard footsteps up in the attic.
Light seems never come.

Josh 7

(I queried the last line. Did he miss out a 'to' perhaps? Josh was quite adamant he liked the poem at it was. Reading it a day or two later, I realised he was right! The poem has more impact with the last four words equally emphasised – light seems never come.)

Anger
I feel as though somebody has reached down inside me,
Wrenching about and pulling.
Words won't come.

Clare 9

Sparrow-Hawk
The hunter of darkness skims the clouds,
Gliding into the night.
No creature is safe.

Alex 9

Model poems

Another very easy way into poetry is to introduce the children to a poem with a simple structure and ask them to write their own versions. It is essential that the conventions of the poem follow a straightforward pattern, so that children can try it out for themselves. Providing model poems can be a first step into poetry or a useful extension of work begun with haiku. With the structure of the poem given, the children are free to concentrate on their ideas and their use of language. I offer six examples, but the possibilities are endless. Just flick through any general anthology and you may find poems that suit you better. It is essential that children *see* as well as hear these model poems.

1 If There Were No Rabbits

If there were no rabbits
I would miss
the rabbit's twitching nose.
I would miss
the soft, silky fur,
the shiny smooth fur,
his ears silky, pointed and smooth
his lovely long wiry whiskers.
It would be so sad to see them go,
his bouncy back legs
and his velvety paws
that he does handstands with.
It would be terrible
not to see them again.
The way a rabbit crunches
carrots and cabbages
with a crunch munch
It would be uncumftabal
without it.
His bobbing tail
like snow, it would be dreadful
without it.

Catherine Browning 7

On this occasion I borrowed a gorgeous rabbit from the local pet shop. We observed him closely, stroked him, listened to his noises, watched him eat. Then we thought about all the things we would miss if there were no rabbits left in the world. The children were advised to take a new line for each item mentioned.

If there were no rabbits ...
I would miss
the long, pointed ears,
the shining blood-red eyes,
the glossy fur
the twitching nose.
If there were no rabbits I would miss
the long thin whiskers,
the lolloping clumsy way they run.

Luke 9

If there were no rabbits I would miss
The razor-blade ears
with white hind legs
and the snowflake nose
But the thing I like most is
the candle-light whiskers
The ruby eyes
The movements remind me of a bouncy ball.

Josh B. 8

Notice how the children spontaneously use metaphor and simile in their poetry without being aware of these conventions. Instinctively they find the images to bring the rabbit to life. Of course the ordinary language of childhood is full of such figures of speech, but in poetry it is highlighted, placed 'up front'. And the simple format of the poem encourages the child to write in 'lines' from the start.

2 What's That Down There?

What's that down there?
What's that moving?
What's that moving down in the dark
   of this chilly black maze of a cave?

Is it Sarallo –
The scarlet snake with the seven
Silver heads
And fangs that snap like a murder trap?

What's that down there?
What's that moving?
What's that moving down in the dark
   of this chilly black maze of a cave?

Is it Farranway —
That back-cracking brute
With a hundred horns
And hoofs that hit like horrible hammers?

What's that down there?
What's that moving?
What's that moving down in the dark
   of this chilly black maze of a cave?

Is it Thilissa —
That slippery wisp of
A whispering ghost of a
Girl who died
In the moistness of mist
Which lies like a shroud on
The underground lake
down in the dark in this chilly black maze of a cave?

Adrian Mitchell

Using this with a group of children tackling poetry for the first time, I emphasise the rhythm and repetitions, the sense of something dark, strange and horrible lurking at the bottom of the cave. Most children used the first three lines of the refrain, then got straight in after 'Is it ... '

What's that down there?
What's that moving?
What's that moving down in the dark?
Is it a black bat
Flying through the dark?

What's that down there?
What's that moving?
What's that moving down in the dark?
Is it a white ghost
Floating through the air?

What's that down there?
What's that moving?
What's that moving down in the dark?
Is it a red flame leaping in the air
Dancing flaming down in the dark?

What's that down there?
What's that moving?
What's that moving down in the dark?
Is it a yellow glow of shining eyes
Staring through the darkness?   *Katherine 9*

(I liked the way Katherine used a different colour in each verse.)

What's that down there?
What's that moving?
What's that moving down in the dark?
Is it a ghost, the ghost of Thomas with
Thin wavy strands of hair and a ghostly figure?

What's that down there?
What's that moving?
What's that moving down in the dark?
Is it an eagle gliding slowly along with
Glittering eyes looking for food?

What's that down there?
What's that moving?
What's that moving down in the dark?
Is it a dragon with green scales down
His back, breathing fire over the walls of a cave?

What's that down there?
What's that moving?
What's that moving down in the dark?
Is it a snake with a red tongue flickering
In the dark, slithering along looking for its home?

What's that down there?
What's that moving?
What's that moving down in the dark?
Oh shut up
stop imagining things!   *Fiona 10*

3 You!

You!
Your head is like a hollow drum.
You!
Your eyes are like balls of flame.
You!
Your ears are like fans for blowing fire.
You!
Your nostril is like a mouse's hole.
You!
Your mouth is like a lump of mud.
You!
Your hands are like drum-sticks.
You!
Your belly is like a pot of bad water.
You!
Your legs are like wooden posts.
You!
Your backside is like a mountain-top.   *Igbo, Africa*

As all of us who work with children know very well, they love to insult one another. It's a sign of friendship! This traditional African poem offers both an opportunity for delicious insults (children must learn not to go over the top – I think that Jamie just avoids this charge) and a form which requires a line for each insult.

Your fingers are like matchsticks
Your Head is like a ping-pong ball
Your brain is like a walnut
Your fingernails are like blades of grass
Your hair is like snakes
Your nose is like a pig's
Your ears are like leaves
Your feet are as bony as a winter tree without leaves
Your hands are like ladybirds
Your body is like a tall skinny pine tree.

Libby 9

Your chin is like a puckered up dog's bottom.
Your stomach is like a bag of wholemeal.
Your eyes are like lumps of sewage waste.
Your eyes are slimy like a worm.
Your nose is like a stilt
Your ears are like double basses.
Your mouth is as big as a blue whale.
Your feet smell like stilton cheese.
Your bottom is like Mount Everest covered in blisters.
Your head is like an elephant.
Your belly button is like a black hole.
Your hair is like an ape's skin.
Your toes are like boulders.
Your knees are like the remains of a world war.
Your fingers are like sausages.
Your brain must be fixed in your head with bostik glue,
I wish you weren't in this world!

Jamie 9

4 Chivvy

Grown ups say things like:
Speak up
Don't talk with your mouth full
Don't stare
Don't point
Don't pick your nose
Sit up
Say please
Less noise
Shut the door behind you
Don't drag your feet
Haven't you got a hankie?

Take your hands out of your pockets
Pull your socks up
Stand straight
Say thank-you
Don't interrupt
No-one thinks you are funny
Take your elbows off the table.

Can't you make your own mind up about anything?

Michael Rosen

Children love this poem. It's so true to life! Once again, it is very easy to construct a poem taking a line for each 'chivvy'. Here is Libby again. Her mother told me she felt quite embarrassed after reading it, as it captured just the sort of things she used to complain about.

Mummy's Orders

Turn the programme off.
Brush your hair.
I'm not finding your slippers for you.
Take that look off your face.
Tidy up your bedroom.
Less noise please, I've a headache.
Stop jumping on your bed.
Time to get up now.
Brush your teeth.
Do something sensible.
Stop crying.
Don't call me from upstairs when I'm downstairs.
Who left the light in the bathroom on?
Put your slippers on.
It's high time you were asleep.   *Libby 9*

5 The Door

Go and open the door.
  Maybe outside there's a tree
  or a wood,
  a garden,
  or a magic city.

Go and open the door.
  Maybe a dog's rummaging.
  Maybe you'll see a face,
  or an eye,
  or a picture
    of a picture.

Go and open the door.
  If there's a fog
  it will clear.

Go and open the door.
  Even if there's only
the darkness ticking,
  even if there's only
  the hollow wind,
  even if
      nothing
          is there,
go and open the door.

At least
there'll be
a draught.

Miroslav Holub

'The Door' is one of my favourite poems. I particularly like the optimism, urging the reader to activity, to look for the unexpected under our noses, to see value in our everyday lives, to day-dream. It encourages us to go out and find experience, to do anything but stay put. It is an opening out poem for children. And there is a clear invitation for every new idea with: 'Go and open the door. Maybe ...'

What follows is a class poem written in response to the original. This was a one-off session with children who were not familiar with poetry. It was an undemanding experience, as they were only asked to make up a line each which I then put together in a poem. There was much discussion about which line should go where, and the children were interested and involved. The poem was a very modest success, but I hope it broke down the pupils' assumptions that poetry was remote and difficult.

Go and open the door –
Maybe outside there's a cuddly lion,
a beautiful princess,
or a dalek saying
EXTERMINATE
EXTERMINATE.

Go and open the door –
There may only be bright stars glimmering
or the black clouds sagging,
or the moon shining down on your door.

Go and open the door –
You might find a wonder world,
It might be dark and dusty,
But go and open the door.

Even if there's only the bongle, tongle, pomple,
We'd just open the door.
Even if there's a mile long snake
Or a martian standing on a spaceship.

Go and open the door –
Even if it's only the sun burning,
Even if it's sunny and lots of flowers out there
Or you find the dazzling rays of the sun.

Go and open the door –
There may be some treasure!
Silver and gold pieces
and you can keep it.
So go and open the door!

Second year juniors, class poem

Model poems using rhyme

Earlier in the chapter, I tried to make a strong case for using free verse rather than rhyme with beginning writers. But once the pupils have gained confidence in the mastery of simple free verse, it can be fun to try out some easily accessible rhyming poems, once again using models. These are poems whose rhyme-scheme and rhythm give a momentum to the composition. The pupil already has a driving rhythm in the model and an appealing idea to play with, she only has to find her own words to fit into the form.

One of the simplest of all must be the variations on the familiar birthday rhyme. We know there are playground versions. Here are two:

> Happy birthday to you
> Boiled eggs and rat stew.
> The cake has gone mouldy
> Happy Birthday to you.   Camilla 9

> Happy Birthday to you
> Hope you get something new
> Something old will not do-oo
> Happy Birthday to you   Joe 9

And there are possible adaptations of Nursery Rhymes:

> Humpty Dumpty sat on a wall
> Humpty Dumpty made himself small.
> Humpty Dumpty then had a great fall.
> All the gnomes and the little grey men
> Said, 'Scrambled eggs for dinner again.'   Claire 10

> Little Miss Muffet
> Sat on her tuffet
> Eating her curry stew.
> When down came a spider
> And sat down beside her
> And told her to look at the view.   Lynne 10

One of Michael Rosen's best loved series of verses are his 'Down behind the dustbin' rhymes which feature in several of his books. Very small children can make up their own orally. And it is not a bad idea to try making up a few with the whole class before children tackle their own, so that they get accustomed to the rhythm and the rhymes.

> 1 Down behind the dustbin
>   I met a dog called Jim.
>   He didn't know me
>   And I didn't know him.   Michael Rosen

> Down behind the dustbin
> I met a dog called Scott
> I asked him where he came from
> But he had forgot.

> Down behind the dustbin
> I met a dog called Patch
> He wanted to get in a baker's
> But he couldn't lift the latch.   First year juniors

2 The Goblin

A goblin lives in our house, in our house, in our house
A goblin lives in our house all the year round.
He bumps
And he stumps
And he thumps
He knocks
And he rocks
And he rattles at the locks.
A goblin lives in our house, in our house, in our house,
A goblin lives in our house all the year round.

Rose Fyleman

The Ghost

A ghost lives in our cellar, in our cellar, in our cellar
A ghost lives in our cellar
Every single day.
He falls and he crawls and
He passes through the walls.
He bangs
And he clangs
And he has rather long fangs.
A ghost lives in our cellar
Every single day.

Alex 6

The Fairy

A fairy lives in my room, in my room, in my room
A fairy lives in my room
And makes magic all the time.
She peeps
And she weeps
And she works until she sleeps.
She winks
And she thinks
And sometimes she drinks.
A fairy lives in my room, in my room, in my room
A fairy lives in my room
And makes magic all the time.

Sophie 7

The poem 'Slowly' by James Reeves is a favourite with many teachers. And children seem to empathise with its quiet, gentle mood. In the first class I ever taught a very gifted eight-year-old wrote this after hearing and seeing the original.

3 Slowly

Slowly the tide creeps up the sand,
Slowly the shadows cross the land.
Slowly the cart-horse pulls his mile,
Slowly the old man mounts the stile.

Slowly the hands move round the clock,
Slowly the dew dries on the dock.
Slow is the snail – but slowest of all
The green moss spreads on the old brick wall.

James Reeves

Slowly the time is trickling away.
Slowly go the hours of midsummer's day.
Slowly the snowdrops cover the ground
Slowly goes the old man making no sound.
Slowly the sun rises up in the sky
Slowly and softly the best way to die.
Slowly the pupil learns the way
Slowly goes time when you've nothing to play.
Slowly you silently sleep and
Slowly you grow every day.

Andrew 8

Finally in this section I want to demonstrate what can be achieved in this mode by a pupil relatively experienced at writing poetry. Here is a teacher describing how the writing was set up:

'Sometimes I read poetry so that it can act as a direct stimulus to children's own poetry writing, as in Holub's poem "Inside a Boy's Head". Not all the children liked the poem, but they were stimulated to talk about their own thoughts. I asked everyone to write down a selection of things which were inside their own heads. I did the same, and after about ten minutes we stopped and discussed our first efforts which were lists of unrelated ideas. I asked the children to think about their poems in preparation for another session later that week.'

Inside a Boy's Head

Inside it there are ...
Purple strangers from the planet Mars
Stereo jukeboxes and big, flash cars and
Exciting films and favourite film stars.

Inside it there is ...
A white knight riding through a fantasy land
Armour on his body, a sword in his hand, and
Playing guitar in a Rock 'n' Roll band.

Inside it there is ...
Thoughts of meeting Mickey Mouse,
Spending the night in a haunted house and
Taking part in a medieval joust.

Inside it there are ...
Trips to the jungle with lions and snakes
Swimming through rivers and stars and lakes – and
Eating one million chocolate cakes.

Inside it there is ...
An impractical design for a flying machine,
What things will be like in the year two thousand and
    eighteen and
Collecting a medal from England's queen!

Adam 10

In this chapter I have tried to demonstrate some straightforward 'starters' for poetry. These are hooks on which children can easily hang simple ideas. Later some may wish to explore more sophisticated kinds of poetry. In the beginning my concern is to make poetry accessible to children, a mode of writing they enjoy undertaking and can manipulate successfully.

Some children will do little more than write simple 'free verse' poems on request. At least they will have mastered one type of writing which will have a positive spin-off for all their language work. Some children experience a deep enjoyment in writing poetry, finding it the best vehicle for self-expression. Others will want to experiment with forms like ballads, tanka, rhyming verse, dialect poetry and the like. Still others will learn to write poems of substance and quality. A very few will publish their poetry in adulthood. All these children will have gained immeasurably from making their own poetry.

'All things counter, original, spare, strange'

(G. M. Hopkins)

5   Finding a theme

Most teachers are conscientious about trying to find suitable subject matter for the writing their pupils undertake. They scour source books and articles, exchange ideas with colleagues and attend likely courses in their search for the perfect theme. The intention, of course, is to find interesting ideas which will galvanise their pupils into successful writing. Many teachers feel that finding a lively theme suited to their particular class is the major preparation for a writing session, followed only by giving an appropriate 'stimulus'. I believe that too many teachers spend too much time searching for ideas for one-off writing sessions. With the best of intentions, we as teachers are imposing our own ideas, usually second-hand ideas, on our pupils.

It is not necessary to think up lots of new, gimmicky ideas to get our pupils writing. In fact, the well-tried topics that have always been the subject matter of poetry are probably as profitable, so long as they are presented in a way that is meaningful to children. What does matter is getting our pupils *involved* in an idea, so that they can get to the heart of it. One could say that the chosen theme for poetry is the shell. For children to write with conviction, they need to break open the shell, getting down to the kernel. To get inside a theme, the poet needs to reach down inside herself for that which is normally out of reach. Each child will pare down a theme in her own way, particularly if it is limited in scope and manageable.

Here is a simple example to illustrate this point. I realise that the categories I am using are crude, but they are recognisable just the same. Let's take the topic of fire:

(a) A 'conventional' approach might include a discussion about fires, hazards, the fire brigade, colours ... the children asked to write a poem about fire. This is too general, there are too many 'vague' ideas, it lacks focus.

(b) A 'lively' approach might be burning some paper in the classroom, eliciting a dramatic reaction from the children who are keen to write about what they've just seen. You may get some lively writing, but it is likely to be limited to the experience.

(c) A 'creative' approach might involve lighting a few candles in a dark room and asking the children to watch closely as the wax dissolves. The children would be encouraged to use their senses and deal with the 'here and now', but also to look for associations. The burning candle, the dying flame tend to become symbolic of other things: life and death; time passing by; youth, hope, energy, vitality; the bible, religion, church; birthdays, festivals; dark and light; what life was like before electricity ... from the ordinary and everyday to the profound. The writers will not consciously conjure up vivid associations; it happens involuntarily when the conditions are right. Time is taken to get the pupils involved; they are encouraged to find meaning in the experience.

Let us consider in more detail what is meant by 'the right conditions' in terms of the pupils, the teachers and the themes themselves.

The pupils

Whenever possible pupils should have the opportunity of selecting their own subject matter for poetry.

The best topics for poetry are often those which encourage our pupils to draw on personal experience. The best themes are already there – in the children.

Pupils will not write the best poetry of which they are capable, unless real engagement with the subject matter takes place.

The teachers

Teachers are inclined to look outside themselves for poetic material by writers far removed from their classrooms in time and space. Often the most profitable themes are right under our noses.

Teachers can develop the confidence to be the initiators of their own ideas or give a fresh slant to ideas gleaned second-hand. The theme will be fresh, if the teacher takes the time to make it his own!

The themes

Perhaps the most important part of presenting an idea for poetry to pupils is finding the means of making it accessible to the group concerned – helping the pupils find a focus – a way in to the particular theme.

Pupils selecting their own themes

Although this is my fundamental belief, I realise that it is ambitious. It is no easy task to get a group of pupils to be responsible for choosing their own subject matter. And it certainly does take time. It might be realistic to suggest that, even for pupils who are encouraged to read and write poetry regularly, who are read to and who have access to a varied supply of anthologies, it might still take as long as six months before the majority has the confidence to write in this way. Just the same, this is my ultimate goal.

No adult poet writes about a given theme because she has been asked or told to. She writes because she has to, about the things which matter to her.

Poets vary enormously in the style and content of their work, but invariably they write because they have been moved in some way. Some incident, experience, reflection or idea sets off a train of thought and a poem will be the end result. However intellectual the ideas, whatever precision in poetic craft is achieved, or even however hilarious the results, poems begin with feeling.

Yet we often ask children to write about things they know and care little about. Of course we try to arouse their interest, but a ten minute introductory 'stimulus' is all that most of us allow. If we do choose a topic the children are familiar with, they may not feel like writing about it when we happen to set the task. We must find the way to give children the maximum opportunity to write about genuine concerns. Hopefully, we can also put behind us the practice of asking our pupils to write about snow on a bright November day, before the first snow of the season has fallen, or to stick to the subject of cats, prepared the night before, on the day the first snow falls! This is an artificial way of writing. Our pupils cannot write with conviction in these circumstances. We all write best about that which excites us now, though often we will be excited because of links with past experience, and that, of course, will be different for each individual in the class. But once children have a reasonable experience of writing poetry, and have gained confidence in their ability to communicate their ideas, poetry can become an automatic mode of expression for some of their writing.

There are private and personal themes within each individual. A good teacher can help the child to see when there is a poem to be written. Once the basic idea of free verse is mastered, a pupil can put feelings and experiences into poetry with relative ease. The occasion may be something special or ordinary in a child's life, something unexpected or confusing, sad, happy or seemingly trivial to an adult. It might be a bike ride, a new baby in the family, the death of a pet, a football match, a birthday.

Here is an example from my own experience. We had a visit from a blind woman with her guide dog one day, as part of a topic on the senses. My class was going to raise money for guide dogs for the blind and our visitor was to provide some background information. As it transpired, the children were only moderately interested in guide dogs, but they were very interested in what it was like to be blind. Searching questions arose. Like most adults in this situation, I wished the children were less direct, less eager to find out all the facts. Our guest was unembarassed and answered their questions with honesty and kindness. When she left several children announced they were going to write poems about blindness. (It should be stressed that we had been writing poetry regularly for several months.) Sarah was one of them. In only a few lines she demonstrates real empathy for what it must feel like to be blind:

Blindness

I don't know what they mean when they say a lovely colour
All the world is dark with blurry brightness,
I grip the handle of my dog and go on.
They say I'm something called blind,
But I can't HEAR any difference
    between me
      and them.   *Sarah 8*

In the type of classroom where children are able to take decisions for themselves, at least some of the time, and have some choice in what they do and when they do it, self-initiated poetry will be of the greatest benefit. A teacher whom the children can trust to find time to read their work seriously and sensitively is also essential.

It will, however, always be appropriate to present an idea for writing poetry to a group of children at some point, particularly in the first few months with a new class, and some teachers will want to continue with this way of working. It is worth remembering that younger and less experienced writers do benefit from being offered a clear topic, with a definite direction from their teachers. But we have not yet moved on to teacher-directed poetry. Let us first look at themes for poetry by concentrating on the children themselves.

The best themes are already inside the children

All serious writing involves introspection, so we want to encourage children to draw on inward experience in their own writing. Much successful poetry comes from dredging up what is already inside us, and presenting it in a unique and personal way. Alan Garner explains the process in relation to writing fiction:

> An isolated idea presents itself. It can come from anywhere. Something seen: something said. It can be an attitude, a colour, a sound in a particular context. I react to it, perhaps forget it, but it is filed away by the subconscious. Later, and there is no saying how long that is, another idea happens involuntarily, and a spark flies. The two ideas stand out clearly and I know that there will be a story.

As teachers we must aim to provide the conditions where a spark can fly. It is not so much a case of providing new experiences, though this has its place and can be useful, but to find a way of setting off old experience in a 'creative' framework. When a pupil engages deeply with a subject, then there is a real pressure to reach down inside herself to say something of significance. Much of this process is unconscious, and the pupil will not be able to stop herself, once embarked on a gripping idea.

How does this happen? Many arguments cited in other parts of the book work towards this end. But on a practical level, pupils are more likely to become 'inspired' in a classroom where poetry is given status and time, where there is a good model in a teacher who reads – and best of all writes – poetry himself, sometimes alongside the children (see chapter 9), where there is a lively collection of anthologies used in a variety of ways, where poetry is regularly read and discussed. One specific strategy is suggested by Ted Hughes in *Poetry in the Making*:

> It can be productive to give out at the beginning of term some of the subjects to be written about during the coming weeks. The pupils would then watch the intervening lessons more purposefully, and we cannot prevent ourselves from preparing for a demand we know is going to be met.

In other words, whether we like it or not, our unconscious takes over, and we begin to anticipate, plan, imagine . . .

On a more mundane level one of the best sources for poetry is classroom life. There is always a craze going on. There are the seasonal ones like conkers, marbles, skipping, cricket. And there are the crazes of the moment – remember skateboards and rubic cubes? We ignore youth culture at our peril. These enthusiasms can be tapped for writing poetry. Here is an example written in the heat of the rubic cube craze:

One .... a frustrating enigma
Two .... a show-off's dream come true
Three ...... a device to cure sanity in anyone
Four .... a torture with the effect
　　　　　 of a brainwasher and a thumbscrew
Five .... a Hungarian professor's revenge on the world
Six .... the only puzzle with a Hungarian Health warning:
　　　　　 you buy one at your own risk

Luke 10

A poem can often be a good way of expressing some aspect of a class project, visit or scientific investigation, as well as preparation for or follow-up to drama, artistic work and so on. Sometimes poetry comes out of other activities. When my class of seven- to eight-year-olds was studying colour, we had made charts, tried 'Impressionist' painting, undertaken experiments and were in the middle of a large frieze based on shades of blue. It seemed logical to look for a slant involving language more directly and poetry was the obvious choice. Colour is very significant in all our lives, so I decided to focus on the children's response to colour, and to find out what particularly excited each individual.

As a preliminary I asked the children to collect red objects over a couple of days, and I displayed some of these on a table covered with a piece of black velvet cloth. We looked at all the various shades and tones of red and discussed our varying reactions to the colour and the images associated with it – blood, roses, sunsets, apples, fire ... Then I read 'What is White?' by Mary O'Neill. I went on to say that each one of us had a special colour and we had to find out which it was. I said this dramatically to create a bit of impact. The children responded positively and very seriously pondered on their special colour. They closed their eyes and concentrated on 'their' colour. I suggested they might hate or love their colour, but they must be strongly drawn to it. We then took a few of the most popular 'special' colours – red, black, gold, silver – and discussed what images we associated with them. As will already be apparent, I often spend a long time in the build-up to writing. Here are some of the results from this session where every child wrote with conviction.

What is Red?

Red is a fire dancing and prancing
Or a red tulip blowing in the wind.
Crying is red running down your face
You want red on top of a windy mountain.
Red is joy crimson joy.
Red is a huge fire all around us.
You can smell red if you sniff in a rose.

Sarah 8

Red is your lips and your blood
And in the valley where tulips grow
And on the apple tree where
rosy apples grow.
My dreams are red when I dream a ladybird.

Hannah 8

What is Black?

Black is the coal that burns fires bright.
Black is the colour that shines at night.
Black is anger, death and sadness.
Black is a nightmare in the dark.
Black is a heart filled with shame.

Katherine 8

What is Silver?
Silver is armour on a bold knight.
Silver is a ghost horse running through the night.
Silver is people locked up in chains.
Silver is water shining at day.
Silver is the rain that comes down at day.
Silver is the sun shining at day.

Ross 8

I have since used this topic on a number of occasions, reading poems like those above to stimulate interest. I have also recommended it as a theme for student teachers. When a student has 'taken on' the theme and made it his own: found his own colour poems, taken a fresh slant, highlighted colour in some novel way, the results are usually good. I have, unfortunately, also been witness to pedestrian poetry lessons on colour. One student gave his third year class a quick exposition on colour entirely from lecture notes, reading the same poem as I had. He then asked the children to write poems about the colour yellow. Readers will not be surprised to find that the pupils were uninspired, writing dull poems about bananas and the sun. Why didn't it work? The student was using second-hand material in a second-hand way. He thought he was on a safe bet that would work with minimum preparation. He did not excite the children, nor did he give them a sense of direction. Writing about 'the colour yellow' is too vague, it lacks direction or interest. He didn't offer them any choice, and his colour wasn't even one likely to stir the emotions. At the end of the lesson, it was clear he blamed me for suggesting colour in the first place! This shows how unimportant is the actual theme compared to the way it is presented to the children.

Another time my class of ten-year-olds was watching a television programme on river life. I thought we might try our hands at watery images, but the children had other ideas. There had been a brief shot of a dead duckling floating upside-down and this was what the children were talking about. Always keen to snatch the moment, I suggested they might attempt an ode to a dead duckling. Off the cuff, I told them a bit about odes (my knowledge was elementary) and they rushed off to write. That night I did some research and found one or two elegies to read to the children. I can't pretend that members of the class later devoted much time and attention to this branch of poetry, but it made me read poetry I hadn't thought about before, the children were interested enough to listen to several odes and it certainly added to the range of poetry covered. Here are a couple of examples, not brilliant, but written with genuine feeling. These two children chose the title by themselves.

Lament for a Dead Duckling

He picked it up and mourned over it
But its soul had gone.
He gently stroked it.
But its soul had gone.
He put it in its nest
But its soul had gone.
Its mother comforted it
But that was no use
Because its soul had gone.

Alice 10

My eyes water as I see
the dead dark duckling floating down
the running river.
Once I had the warm ducking
    in my hands
But now he is cold
    and dead.

Moira 10

I would never actually choose 'death' as a theme for poetry writing. But in this case it came up naturally and unexpectedly, captured the children's attention and therefore seemed appropriate.

To sum up this section concentrating on the pupils:

• We want pupils ultimately to become the initiators of their own poetry.
• Whenever possible, we want children to become deeply involved with their chosen theme, so that they write with purpose and conviction.
• Bearing in mind that a large element in the creative process is unconscious, we want to create a classroom environment where children can take the time to let ideas develop in a natural way.
• The best themes are often based on personal experience and things close to us.

Now for the teachers:

Good themes are often right under our noses!

I have already alluded to using the children and their experiences for writing poetry, and later in this chapter we will look at how teachers can use their own interests and enthusiasm for poetry. But we don't need to look far away to find suitable topics. They are all around us. For the moment let us restrict ourselves to school life as the subject matter for poetry. There is so much potential here.

First of all there is the school building itself. However old and shabby or new and featureless, each person in the institution will have a strong reaction to it and will probably view it in a different way. Take one particular city school with which all the authors have a connection. The old school was an extremely ugly and undistinguished Victorian building with many in-conveniences: a small hall with rough floorboards giving rise to nasty splinters, classrooms up flights of stairs, outside toilets which froze in winter, high windows letting in little light and no room for a library. The present school is very pleasant, built round a quadrangle with lots of flowers, grass, a covered play area, a large playground, and plenty of colour and light. You might think that everyone would welcome the change. Not so – parents missed the character of the old buildings, some children were attached to the old school because it was homely and familiar, one or two of the teachers yearned for the privacy of classrooms tucked away from inquisitive eyes. Most staff and children preferred the new school, but for all sorts of varied reasons. When a teacher asked his fourth years to write about memories of the old school, each child had something different to say. The school was not simply a place, it was a receptacle for a whole set of memories and feelings which could be explored in poetry.

Then there are the school grounds, changing with the time of year. Even an urban school has its wildlife, be it a scrap of wasteground, a few weeds, some insects or the school cat. What can the children see from the playground or from the classroom window?

And what about the children who went to the school in the past? Where are they now? Do they leave anything of themselves behind?

There are plenty of people in a school besides the pupils and teachers. There are cleaners, cooks, secretaries, catering staff, the caretaker. Parents will be in and out of the school and, possibly, other members of the local community. There will also be the special visitors like the road-safety police officer, students, advisers, perhaps even writers. All these people bring something to the life of a school which can be harnessed for writing.

Re-inventing the wheel

No matter what exciting idea we present to our pupils, it will appear lacklustre and unconvincing unless we are genuinely enthralled by it too. And it is not just enthusiasm that is called for. We need to take the time to get 'inside' a theme, so that we can offer something both attractive and accessible to our pupils. Unless we do this they remain other people's ideas and this will be conveyed to our pupils. If a teacher is simply going through the motions, the pupils pick this up, are unstirred and mostly uninspired and this will be reflected in the quality of their writing. In judging poetry competitions for children I have found that, in a few cases, every piece of work from a class of children was interesting – from the naturally very talented writer to the least able child. But other classes writing on the same topic, often from schools in privileged areas, produced poetry that was dull and predictable from virtually every child. It seems likely that the discrepancy in performance among different groups of children had to do with the role of the teacher in fostering real engagement with the subject in hand.

So how, you may well ask, do you get inside a theme? First of all you give yourself time to let ideas grow. You mull them over, find connections and connotations that are your own. Remember introspection is required in teaching as well as learning. Some ideas will need plenty of time to develop, others will 'click' because you know you must sort it out for the next day at school. If the lesson has to be ready for tomorrow, you will cobble something together. If there is less pressure and you really want the theme to work, don't worry if it does not come together right away. Often time will do the work for you, and not necessarily when you are consciously thinking about it. Your subconscious will be trying to solve it for you. Alternatively, some really strenuous thinking is called for at times. Brainstorming with colleagues can be productive on occasion.

One useful method is to ask yourself some questions. Let's take a well-known topic like kites.

- Why did the idea of kites attract me in the first place?
- Did I do some wonderful kite-flying as a child? Did I never get a kite or always want a kite?
- What do I like about them?
- Or do I dislike kites intensely because mine never flew while everyone else's seemed to soar into the air with ease?
- Have I time to have a quick go at kite-flying? (That will be the quickest way to answer all these questions)
- Do I know a good story or poem about a kite?
- Do I have access to some exciting pictures of kites?
- Is it actually kites that interest me or is it the colours, the notion of flying, the idea of belonging to earth and sky?

This should get the ideas flowing. Later, in preparation for poetry, you can ponder the topic from the pupils' point of view. The questions will be of a different order.

- How can I get the children excited about kites?
- What support material will be best for my class?
- Shall we make a kite first? Would this link in with maths or the class project?
- How best can I tackle kite-flying with a class of thirty-five?
- Is this a one-off lesson or should it develop over several days?

Whenever possible teachers should develop their own ideas

Finding a theme for poetry is really very easy. The simplest way is to leaf through an anthology of poetry until you come to a poem that attracts your attention. It is, of course, essential to have some varied and inviting anthologies around you when preparing for poetry. This is your greatest resource. (See appendices 1 and 2 for suggestions). It might be a poem you have always loved, a poem you've been meaning to look at more closely, a poem with terrific appeal to children, a poem that would tie in with the story you are reading to the class, a poem that just happens to chime in with the way you are feeling at the moment. A different teacher would opt for a different poem, and so would you another day. This poem is right for you now, at this moment. You select it intuitively and casually, but it feels right.

You may find that you want to sink into the poem and let its ideas simmer. Alternatively, the poem may lead you to other thoughts. However long this phase lasts, you will be mulling over possibilities for using the poem with your class. What you are searching for is a focus or an angle to help each individual find her own way into the subject. This is very important, because if a child fails to get inside the topic, only superficial writing will follow. I am not suggesting you offer the children a nice, pat formula for writing, but that you open up strands of possibility.

Finding the right questions to arouse pupils' interest is a skilled task. Poets invariably are good at it: they are practitioners in the craft of poetry and they constantly ask themselves searching questions. These are not just the customary questions that we are all so familiar with, about the look, sound, touch and shape of things. We need questions to forge commitment. For example, when the poet Clive Wilmer was working with my pupils on birds, he asked very simply what makes birds different from humans? In what ways are they the same as humans? When I observed Adrian Mitchell working with a class of top juniors on the same theme, I came in to find twenty 'birds' flapping their wings. Adrian had taken them for a flight! But first he asked if they could feel their beaks, their clawed feet, their feathers growing.

Here is an example of a poem about a bird, written by a child who had engaged with the subject:

The Making of a Bird

The delicate tools
The body is carved into shape
The wing is formed with great care
Then the eye
The startled eye
Looking around, waiting, watching.

The sharp beak,
Ready to pick out worms from the soft earth.
The feathers are formed,
And applied with a steady hand.
The bird is made
It watches me for a second
Then flies into the distant skies.

Teresa 9

On another occasion the children were asked to write about bubbles. Of course, they wrote descriptively about what the bubbles looked like, how they moved. But what got them thinking was the question, 'What is a bubble? This sphere of air and water that lasts for a second and is gone?' Finding questions that engage your pupils is by no means automatic: you may need to spend some time thinking about it. The aim is to get the children thinking in a fresh way, to open new doors. When I asked children to write about themselves recently, I told them I wasn't interested in their appearance, but only who they were on the inside. What made them different from everyone else?

If I got my message across, the children were certainly not going to write superficial poems. The questions I'd asked were challenging, even risky to write about. Not everyone wants to look closely inside to tell the world about special bits of themselves, good and bad. But I knew my group and that they needed a challenge. Later several volunteered that it was the best topic they had tackled. What follows will give you a taste of what was achieved that day. You will note they are not all serious. The first poem is by a child who was a sophisticated and able poet and had been working on poetry for several years. The other two examples are more in line with what one would expect from a typical classroom poetry session.

There is in me

There is in me a scorpion
Of malevolence and discretion
Spiteful words and uncontrollable zest.

There is in me a welling fountain
Of self pity and sorrow
Waking fresh from a dream.

There is in me a curtain
Thick and impenetrable
Which I can pierce when I wish.

And there is in me a star
Of contentment and satisfaction
Of growing, living things.

Jessica S. 11

I am the recorder player
Who toots all day
Then finds the end to stop
Because it gets boring

I am the dancer
Who twirls about
Then jumps in the air
And lands in the splits.

I am the gymnast
Who stands on her head
And then collapses.

Jessica R. 9

Me!

Inside me there is a dragon
as fierce as the devil's heart.
When I'm mad
his eyes light up with fury,
breathing fire, grinning teeth.
When I'm sad
he lies there, head in claws
weeping.
When I'm thinking
the dragon sits there, working things out
on that computer in his head.
When I sleep the dragon puts
his weepy head to rest.

Stuart 10

There are other ways to find our own themes. We are always feeling strongly about something: it might be the weather, an item on the news, a local issue, family matters. The arts constantly present us with challenges: films, plays, novels, programmes on television, music. We might be excited by watching or taking part in sport, dancing or amateur dramatics, or enjoy walking, the countryside, foreign travel. All these things and much more make us the complicated people we are – and we can use them in the classroom for poetry.

One night I went to hear Elaine Feinstein reading from her *Euridice* collection. The poetry was based on the myth of Orpheus and Euridice, but explored in terms of the relationship between men and women. I was moved by the human frailty in the poems, Orpheus's inability to resist temptation when he was so close to his goal. A feminist and a poet, Elaine Feinstein naturally concentrated on the reactions of the woman, doomed finally to a hopeless living death after being let down by her man. I was also mesmerised by the vision of Hades, the tortures more subtle and terrible than physical violence.

How could I use it with children? I reread the myth in a well-written version for children and asked their reactions. How did they think the various characters would feel? What was the saddest part of the story? Did it have anything to do with us living in the eighties? For the first and last time children wrote poems for me with titles like Hell. I encouraged them to go with whatever part of the story they wanted to explore in poetry. What had moved them? For some it was that dreadful underground hell, perhaps a metaphor for the dark and fearful things in life. Others like me were intrigued by the waste. Why couldn't Orpheus have restrained himself? A few were caught up in Euridice's plight. How would she feel about Orpheus now – forgiving, vindictive, despairing? The first example cited is, I think, a profound and disturbing poem, especially the last three lines.

Hell

Hell.
A place in the depths below the surface of the Earth,
A place occupied only by the ghosts of people
Lost to the human world.
Sometimes known as Hades it is ruled by Pluto,
A savage barbarian with a heart of stone.
It would be impossible to give a full description of Hell,
As no one has ever come back from it.
But it is probably a place riddled with fire
And the ashes of burnt out ghosts
For even ghosts can crumble   *Luke 11*

Lost

Orpheus looked back; he had lost her.
When you die you have lost your life.
Ixion had lost joy,
Tantalus lost hope,
Sisyphus lost strength.

Hate loses love,
Buying loses money,
Sleep loses tiredness,
Fear loses courage,
Joy loses sorrow.

Only in heaven there is no loss.   *Zac 12*

The strength of these poems reminds us of the power of old, old stories to cast their spells on children.

Some themes which always seem to work

There are some themes that always seem to strike a responsive chord in children. There are numerous possibilities, but I've chosen a few ideas that children and teachers have cited repeatedly.

Animals are an obvious choice, but some work better than others for poetry. (There will always be the exceptions to this rule with gifted teachers and children.) Cats, bats, tigers, insects, snakes, and to a lesser extent horses and mice, hold a fascination that can be well expressed in poetry, whereas I find dogs, sheep and cows do not. Birds are marvellous, of course. The time of day, time of year, annual festivals, the weather offer enormous scope. Night, darkness, the moon, stars, night fears, dreams, nightmares ... are always gripping, as indeed are all the elements.

I have already stressed that everyday life is full of promise, its high as well as its low spots. Michael Rosen's poetry reminds us how entertaining conversations, quarrels, school and family incidents, jokes, confusions ... can be. The natural world is a consantly changing resource. Going out on walks and visiting places can be suggestive, as can the opportunity to look closely at and handle real things – ancient artefacts borrowed from a museum, empty egg shells, feathers, pieces of driftwood, a dead flower. Pictures and music make an evocative stimulus for poetry. Stories can work wonderfully. And we have already talked about using poems themselves. Some abstract themes can be productive too – peace, anger, delight, drawing on the emotions. Whatever the theme, children can employ their senses, their feelings.

To conclude this chapter, here is how an age-old theme was used in a personal way:

'It was September, the beginning of term with a new class. The weather was fine, the school hall was polished, the walls were bare and the children came to school with new clothes and new aspirations. I hardly knew the names of all the children, but I knew I wanted them to write something, preferably something "poetic", by the end of our first week together. That first week of term presented me with so many lists to fill in: "remedial" group, dinner registers, attendance registers, those who would help with getting out apparatus, chairs for assembly ... The lists went on and on. The beginning of the school year was always like this for fourth years. They were growing up, taking responsibilities, changing. I had seen this class as seven-year-olds gradually maturing. Now they had reached their final year in junior school. In the middle of one of these interminable lists I stopped. Did they like doing these jobs? Why did teachers expect them to do more now? We began talking about maturing, responsibility, the autumn term, being the oldest children in the school.

The children had so much to offer in the discussion. I told them I had been watching them grow for three years. I mentioned little ways in which I had noticed they had changed. They did the same, remembering different hair styles, clothes, losing teeth, gaining freckles! It was a delightful session, full of lively, perceptive comments. The more we talked the more they remembered about how they had changed. Autumn terms and their changing lives were linked together. I wanted to use their perceptions and feelings as the basis for a poetry lesson, but I resisted the temptation to begin immediately. It was autumn, I could gather a richer harvest by first sowing a few more seeds of my own. The following day I read the children verses from "Ecclesiastes" and played the song "For every season, there is a time ..." I showed pictures of babies and old people, contrasted ripe apples with wrinkled apples, read the famous "All the world's a stage ..." speech from *As You Like It* and Ted Hughes' poem "There Came a Day" from *Season Songs*. At the end of all this preparation I called the children together and we talked again, recalling the things we had been thinking about over the week. One by one the children left the group, went back to where they felt most comfortable and began to write. They were quiet and after half an hour I asked them to share with everyone else what they had been writing.'

Julian wrote:

Changes
Everything changes
People, trees,
All nature's things change.
Milk turns sour,
Apples go bad,
Wheat turns ripe.

> As time goes by
> A queer phrase, time changes
> Everything.
> A book fades
> A painting shows age
> Coals burn, fires die
> All things change –
> In time.

You go back to
An old house. It has changed –
Not much, but still it has
Changed.
A once fiery stallion
Now an old tired horse
Everything changes –
In time.

Julian 11

6 The Ancient Mariner – a poetry project

In the autumn of 1984 I began teaching a group of children who had recently been grouped together to form a class of fourth year juniors. After an initial settling period the children began to work well together. Their writing was honest and uninhibited. I was very aware of the potential of these particular children, as individuals and as a group. I had been working with the class for a few weeks when I began to think I would like to do something special with them – something a bit different which would make demands upon the children and greater demands upon me. By now it was half-term and, although I had been quite consciously looking for some project that would inspire me, nothing had really presented itself as being the right thing. It was during the half-term holiday that an idea did occur to me. The school is on the National Theatre's mailing list and I was idly browsing through the programme of forthcoming events when I noticed that Michael Bogdanov was producing 'The Rime of the Ancient Mariner' at the Olivier Theatre. Perhaps this was the answer. Perhaps I could use this poem as the basis for the sort of ideas I wanted to explore with my class. During the holiday I kept returning to the actual text of the poem and found myself thinking of ways in which individuals and groups could work.

By the time the holiday was over I was eager to return to the children and put this proposition to them. On my way to school, I recalled the children's faces, conjuring them as individuals and then as a group. In my mind's eye I saw thirty ten-year-olds wreathed in smiles, their eyes shining with expectation as I broke the news of this already-planned project based on a lengthy narrative poem. As I entered the school building I pictured thirty eager hands wildly clamouring for a place on the coach to go and see an old sailor telling a story about a dead bird! Oh, misguided teacher, enthusiastic and well-intentioned, but wrong! Just how wrong and how much I had to learn was about to be revealed. The first day back after the holiday I had the misfortune to be on break duty. My rosy picture of smiling innocent childhood soon faded as I separated Jason and David as they disputed the rightful ownership of a plastic toy soldier. After marshalling two hundred children into various doorways on a cold wet morning I was still, surprisingly, keen to meet my own class and reveal my latest project to them. Removing my own coat in the children's cloakroom I overheard their animated conversation about the previous week's activities. Many of them had visited interesting places and there was much to talk about, but I was struck by the somewhat impoverished diet of television programmes. Some of the children were keen to catch up on the latest affair in the current soap operas, others were anxious to know about some recent struggle in the 'A-Team'.

I realised then that, as it stood, 'The Ancient Mariner' project could not really compete with their modern stories. If the children were going to get anything out of this idea, I had to sell it to them. Telling them about it would not be enough. The reasons for going to the National Theatre had to be *their* reasons. The motivation for the work and the visit had to come from the children themselves. I was confident that, once enthusiastic, they would find ways of developing the work but I knew that I had to set up a situation which would capture their imagination and allow their ideas to flourish. So that day I said nothing about my plans. I listened carefully to their conversation at break-times and consciously spent time re-establishing my relationship with them and their relationship with one another. However, my confidence in the children prompted me to risk sending for the tickets that evening. I couldn't afford to wait for their response. I imagined them eventually wanting to go and all the tickets being sold out. I 'phoned a teacher friend and asked if she wanted to share with her class the visit to the theatre and the risk of paying for the tickets and the coach. I managed to persuade her and the following day we sent our cheques and our ticket requirements off to the National Theatre box office. If we hadn't managed to persuade the children to join us, we would owe the National Theatre a lot of money!

I began working on the children the very next day. We were in the school hall, having finished drama work. I had deliberately stopped the session a few minutes early and, while the children were pulling on sweaters and tying up shoelaces, I played a track from a John Denver record. The song is called 'Darcy Farrow' and tells the sad story of a young bride who drowns in the local river. Some of the children were especially interested and affected by the story and wanted to hear it again. After the second hearing I asked them if they knew other songs which told stories. I was surprised at their response. They knew a wide variety, some were modern pop songs, others more traditional folk tunes. I invited them to bring in any they particularly liked. I listened to them all before I shared them with the class. We then discussed what we liked about such songs and what we didn't like. Some of the children had brought along traditional sea shanties sung by The Spinners and these were popular. Almost everyone liked them, and I talked to the group about the nature of such songs and why they should tell stories.

The conversation was wide-ranging and began to touch on the nature of story-telling and its function. I was impressed by the children's perceptive observations about their own use of story-telling. Inevitably, the conversation included television viewing. We discussed the appeal of popular soap operas. I also read part of 'The Otterbury Incident' by C. Day Lewis and discussed why we all wanted to know what happened next. Then I played tapes of people who were good story-tellers. At breaktime some of the children read stories to the infants. We talked about this experience and about my experiences as a student teacher reading to secondary school groups. I reminded them of a recent incident in an assembly, when an infant vociferously disputed that pigs live in brick cottages! My class of fourth years had witnessed this and we were able to discuss their ability to suspend disbelief. Infants are, at times, unable to do this. We discussed Jackanory presentations and radio and television dramatisations of children's stories. I talked to the children about people I knew who could tell marvellous stories about everyday events. Some of the children gave examples of relations or neighbours who told riveting tales. Some children suggested that class members were very good at telling a tale! I played a tape of ghost stories to get the children to think about the extraordinary spell that can be woven when a good story is well told.

All these discussions and activities, which had arisen after listening to the John Denver track, had taken place over a period of about ten days. It was getting uncomfortably close to the theatre date and I still had said nothing about the proposed visit. Time was running out but I continued to say nothing. By now the children were tuned in to narrative. During poetry reading sessions in class I read 'The Gresford Disaster' and the children began to look for other poems that told a story. Sometimes individual children would read them to the class, at other times a group would read so that the pace and tone of the poems could be varied. There was a great diversity of poetry and of renderings. These story-telling poetry sessions became an important part of the day. I usually timed them to take place just before lunch so that, should questions or ideas arise from the poetry, there would be time in the afternoon to deal with them properly.

During one particularly cold lunchtime a group of children came to me and asked if they could stay in class. I told them that I would be busy putting up a display but they could stay in and help if they liked. The display was to draw the children's attention to the text of some of the narrative poems we had talked about. I had collected magazine pictures which depicted modern disasters, for example earthquakes, wars, volcanic eruptions, air crashes, car accidents. I had also reproduced the texts of part of the songs and poems we had read. The children were very interested and, as others entered the classroom to collect coats or packed lunch boxes, there was quite a gathering around the display.

That afternoon I asked the children to illustrate either one of the poems we had recently heard or to draw the kind of disaster which moved men and women to respond in poetry or in song. The resulting artwork was, in itself, quite moving. Many of the children had drawn pictures of starving children and hopeless parents. Others had drawn scenes from the First and Second World Wars. One child drew a lifeboat in a stormy sea, another painted a newly dug grave with a small figure of a bride in the corner of the picture. All the artwork told me something about each artist. I began to feel that I had now firmly established the link between poetry and story-telling. The children's artwork made me believe that they could now receive a long, narrative poem as something quite natural and quite acceptable. I had just over a week to go before I needed to collect the money for the tickets. It was Friday evening. I would introduce the poem on Monday and hope the story would weave its own spell.

I had chosen to read 'The Rime of the Ancient Mariner' from the Chatto and Windus edition with illustrations by Mervyn Peake. I had two reasons for this. One was that the text was clearly and simply set out on the page. My second reason was the extraordinary haunting quality of the drawings themselves, which were placed appropriately and boldly throughout the book. I know that the designer of the set in the National Theatre production had been strongly influenced by Gustave Doré's illustrations and I managed to get a copy of this attractive book, although the children preferred the Mervyn Peake.

I had told adjacent classes that I was going to introduce the poem and that I did not want any interruptions, if possible, for about an hour. I asked the children to put a 'Do Not Disturb. Poetry in Progress' sign on the door, collected everyone together in our reading corner and sorted out who was to sit on which cushion with whom. They were settled and, I hoped, as receptive to such literature as I could make them. It was now up to me to read the poem as well as possible, pausing for their responses and my explanations. I actually spent about five minutes showing the book itself, talking about the cover, the title, the size, the print, the publisher, the author and a little about the poem, not too much here because I wanted the language of the poetry to speak for me. Everyone got comfortably arranged. For some this meant lying down, for others leaning against each other. One or two of the children preferred to sit on their own, nearby but at their desks. I sat in a small armchair with three children on cushions near my feet. Most of them closed their eyes automatically ready to watch 'the film going on in their head'. I use this phrase quite deliberately before I read to children, believing that the camera work and techniques of modern film have influenced the way in which visual images appear in children's minds. I usually ask them to recall a certain scene from their film, and some of their descriptions would win Oscars if translated into the medium of the cinema.

I began to read and to weave the spell that only good stories can weave. I spent an hour on the first session, reading, talking, listening, explaining, re-reading and questioning. It was an exciting session with the children. All of them took part, some more involved with the artwork than with the language of the poetry, but all responding to images that were potent and deeply felt. We stopped for lunch and returned to read the second half of the poem. We spent the rest of the afternoon talking, exchanging ideas and listening to one another. They kept referring to the text and half-remembered phrases were repeated by children whose own language was quite limited. At the end of the afternoon I knew that I could suggest the visit to the National Theatre and that they would all want to go. I showed them the publicity for the production and told them that I was going to see it. The most unlikely enthusiast of narrative poetry said 'Lucky devil!' and I invited him to join me. This caused an outburst of protest from the others and I suggested to them that really they might not like it, that it might not be as good as their own productions inside their heads. But they were insistent and I promised them that I would ring up and see if there were any remaining tickets. The children left school in twos and threes, some of them talking about the sailing ships of that era, others wondering how big an albatross's wingspan was. Another asked me what I thought the 'thousand, thousand slimy things' really were. The questions had arisen from the children's interest, which meant that they would be motivated to work towards the answers. The work we would do would arise from their enquiry and interest and they would suggest the next stage of our work on the poem.

The following day, two children had arrived in my classroom at twenty past eight with the money for their tickets. After much questioning I revealed that we could go and the children were so excited they could hardly be controlled before it was time for morning assembly. Because there were only a few days to go before the visit, there was an air of feverish excitement about the entire enterprise. I wanted to begin some artwork before we went, because I wanted to see how the poetry and the Mervyn Peake drawings had influenced the children. Quite naturally the collage groups were formed, some working on the wedding scene, others on the storm, others on the ghosts, a group of three working entirely on the construction of a ghost ship. The children worked hard, hammering out ideas, suggesting different art techniques – tie-dye sails, crêpe paper skeletons, spatter paint backgrounds, a papier-mâché albatross. For two days they measured and cut and glued and painted. The classroom was transformed into a workshop and I was the manager, guiding, suggesting, directing – and sometimes arbitrating. Throughout the progress close reference was made to the text of the poem. It was an exciting time and, as work was finished and displayed, the classroom began to resemble the set of a production. We were only about half-way through all this when the great day arrived.

At a quarter to two we waited expectantly in the foyer of the Olivier Theatre and were delighted when a troupe of actors, guests at the wedding feast, surrounded us all. Dancing and playing instruments, they led us into the theatre to our seats, jumped onto the stage and the play had begun. The children were enthralled, by turns fearful, apprehensive, wary. They were delighted with the sailors' humour, their songs and feats of agility. They were in awe of the sailor who dropped twenty feet from the rigging of the ship to hang lifeless as the relentless sun beat down upon the deck. Some were genuinely saddened as the graceful albatross sank to the ground, killed by the crossbow. They were afraid of the figure of Death and his ghastly companion. It was a memorable day and we all returned home enriched by the experience and stimulated to continue our own exploration of the poem.

This we did in a variety of ways. The collage work continued and was erected in the classroom. It covered every available space and we used the ceiling too. The children talked for a long time about the production and, as their most immediate visual recollections faded, I brought them back to the text to examine the poetry more closely. A great deal of work was in progress by this time, the beginning of December. Some children chose to investigate the albatross, its habitat, feeding habits; some researched the superstitions which surrounded a sailor's life, especially at that time, and studied the history of sailors and the conditions of a sailor's life. Others investigated sailing ships and made balsa wood models complete with ghostly lights and tiny skeletons hanging from the mast and rigging. Two girls made a collection of sea-shanties and wrote out the words with illustrations. Some of the children tried to write their own sea-shanties, others wrote poetry about ghosts and mysteries at sea.

The children's curiosity was insatiable and their capacity for work was outstripping mine as the term hurried to a close. Their enthusiasm for this work did not appear to wane. It was rekindled when, about a week after our visit, as the children were giving me a character description of the Ancient Mariner himself, I asked them if they thought he was to blame for what happened. Not one child spoke immediately. There was silence for a few seconds and then they all spoke at once, all justifying different viewpoints. In the ensuing shouting one voice was heard above the others. 'Bring him to court!' it shouted. And that is just what we did. We enacted 'The Trial of the Ancient Mariner'. All around us infants and juniors alike were making stars and angels and my class was engaged in a moral wrangle over a dead albatross. Even Christmas had to wait this year. I set up the situation by inviting contenders for the various roles. Our cast was as follows:

The Ancient Mariner	The pilot's boy
Two sailors (back from the dead)	A secretary
The Hermit	A bride
Death	A groom
Life-in-Death	Counsel for the prosecution
A doctor	Counsel for the defence
An albatross (back from the dead)	A policeman
A judge	3 wedding guests
A senior judge	2 clerks of the court
A jury (we had 10 in ours)	A newspaper reporter

Each day the court met at certain times. These were posted in advance on the classroom door by the clerk of the court, e.g. 'Court in session: 11 a.m. tomorrow. All please attend.' During the hearing we had large notices which said, 'No smoking, no radios and no admittance once the judge has arrived.' We listened to everyone's evidence although the court became somewhat rowdy with uncontrolled laughter when the albatross and the bride had a difference of opinion while waiting to give evidence. There were newspaper reports of the day's proceedings with headlines like 'Fresh evidence of victimization – A. M.'s friends give more clues in Albatross mystery.' The trial lasted a week, with the judge and jury constantly referring to the text of the poem to verify points. We began the trial in a light-hearted manner but, as the time went on, it became clear that it was gaining in importance and there was an atmosphere of tension. 'Who do you want to win?' 'Do you think he's guilty?', I was often asked but I aligned myself with the judge and jury and said we couldn't discuss the case. The jury came to ask for separate break-times because they were supposed to keep away from the witnesses. For two days I sat with the judges and jury at lunch times so that we could sift through the evidence. Friday came and with it the final court hearing. It was a very tense moment when the jury returned a verdict of 'Not guilty'. The Ancient Mariner was carried shoulder high around the classroom and the newspaper reporters and media crews surrounded him. It was three days before the end of the Christmas term. The Ancient Mariner had triumphed in more ways than one.

That night I left my classroom late. As I turned off the lights I noticed that there was a small glow from one of the balsa wood ships. I walked over to disconnect the wires and I noticed that someone had managed to remember that we hadn't decorated for Christmas. Life-in-Death was grasping a cardboard model of a Christmas pudding!

7 Helping with technique

Take no thought of the harvest
But only of proper sowing.

T. S. Eliot

A healthy diet

By far the best way to help children improve their writing technique is to provide them with plenty of poetry. This seems rather obvious – and it's something we've said before – but it should not be overlooked here. I believe that there are ways of tackling the practicalities of poetry writing, ways which go beyond the provision of a healthy diet, but something needs to be said about the diet first.

Just as you best learn to swim by getting into the water, or develop an appreciation of music by actually listening to it, you can learn most about poetry through a similar immersion. If your children write plenty of poetry, and read or hear plenty of poetry by themselves and others, the quality of their work is bound to improve, and the improvement is fairly painless. Children pick up technical know-how without realizing that they are doing it. The fact that it is painless, a subconscious way of learning, is also important because it means that a child will not try to include techniques for the sake of including them. Asking children to write a poem, while at the same time making them aware of rhyme, rhythm, imagery etc., can lead to poems being distorted by what goes into them. It's rather like pushing packages into a Christmas stocking: the stocking certainly looks as if it is full of interesting things but it has somehow ceased to look like a proper stocking. It has become something else, a container or some kind of wrapping. Bowlers with a natural ability to move the ball can lose that ability if pushed through the coaching manual and made to think about the technical elements of what they are doing. In other words, too great an emphasis on practicalities can stifle creativity. This is why I suggest, later on, that the more detailed teaching of techniques is done through games, rather than in the full-blooded struggle to create a poem. I want to avoid building up a sense of obligation in children, that their writing should contain certain things, or look or sound a particular way. It is better that a child should be engrossed in what she is writing than in the way she writes it.

Plenty of poetry does not, in this case, mean simply a great deal of poetry. It means plenty of variety as well. It's easy enough to discover the sorts of poems that 'go' well in a class – humour and nonsense are usually successful – but the temptation to keep up a steady supply of the same thing should be resisted. In the same way, one would avoid giving children a diet made up entirely of jelly, purely on the grounds that it goes down well. Children need to encounter different forms, intentions and linguistic styles in poems.

Of course, one of the problems of providing this healthier diet is that some poems are much harder to digest than others. They will appear to 'fail' with a class, at least compared with their flashier brethren. They are not immediately accessible and do not work on a single reading. However, we do not want to find ourselves saying, 'I tried Ted Hughes once and they all sat there like puddings so I'm going back to Spike Milligan tomorrow'. Instead we must give some consideration to the presentation of the more difficult and demanding sorts of poems.

This is a complete subject in itself, and really beyond the aims of this book, but I'd like to take a little time to say something about it now because it is relevant to this business of providing a healthy diet. Needless to say, it isn't good enough to read a poem over and over, merely because it is difficult, but a poem re-read after a brief discussion will become more meaningful to children.

All poems, difficult or not, gain from active promotion by an enthusiastic teacher. For example, a teacher might notice, in the middle of a painting session, how a picture begins to remind him of a line from a poem. The poem must mean enough to the teacher to lodge in his head, and his relationship with his children must be such that he can say, 'Doesn't this remind you of ... ?' without sounding as if he planned the remark the night before. The trick is to become so immersed in poetry, so familiar with it that it crops up at odd moments in the ordinary day. And, of course, it's not really a trick. It requires time and effort, though we think that it's time and effort which is not only rewarding but enjoyable as well.

So what are the ingredients of a good poetic diet? We need to offer poems which vary in:

1. **Intention**: poems which are humorous, yes, but also poems which aim to tell a story, poems which question or argue, poems which describe or celebrate, poems which examine emotions.

2. **Linguistic style**: poems which use simple language directly, poems which use a more complex and highly-wrought language, poems which use demotic language, poems which use the language of other times (e.g. Shakespeare) or other places or cultures.

3. **Form**: poems which don't rhyme and poems which do, poems which use different rhyme schemes, poems which use regular rhythms and those which don't, long poems, short poems, poems set out in varieties of line length, stanza length, and which make a variety of patterns on the page,

poems which go with music, poems which don't, poems which might. (see chapter 2). It may seem obvious to add this but it is a good idea to point out to the children the sort of poem you are reading, rather than simply relying on the poem to do all the work. For example, 'This is a poem from the Caribbean. Can you tell from the words it uses? You might notice that it has the first and last line of each stanza rhyming and there are six stanzas...'

Let us now turn to some of the practical activities we can bring to bear in this matter of writing technique, activities which go beyond the provision of a healthy diet. Most of these are preparatory activities, things that can be done apart from the business of writing poems. They are the poet's version of sketching or doodling. The artist who makes many drawings of hands, for instance, finds hands less of a problem when he or she wants to make sure that the hands in the main work are properly done. I want to say something about:

- Preliminaries – a few considerations on what to do before starting to write a poem.
- The elements of poetry – some games and activities which focus on particular poetic techniques.
- Tackling a poem – what to do when the games are set aside, with some remarks on children who find writing difficult (see also chapter 9).

Preliminaries

Chapter 3 and part of chapter 4 deal with the writing process and make some suggestions about preparing to write. However it is worth adding something on the subject here, since a clear and well thought-out approach to writing may help to prevent some technical difficulties from arising. If, before a child sets about creating a poem, she gives some thought to what she intends to write, she is in a better starting position than she would be if she plunged in cold. Obviously, these considerations do not apply to the games, sketches and doodles I'll be discussing next, but to attempts to carve out a 'real' poem.

a)   What do you *intend* to write? Spend a little time thinking about this. What do you want your poem to be about? Don't be content with too vague a title, like 'A Tree', but try to be more precise. Do you want to describe a tree? Or say what it makes you think of? Or to write about the way you're feeling, using the image of a tree as a way in? The intention can and often does change in the writing but it does help to have an idea of what you might like to do in the first place.

b)   What *tone of voice* will you use? Does what you want to say about your tree (or whatever) require you to say it in an easy way, the way you talk? This is often the best way because it is less strained and more honest. You may, however, choose words which sound more musical and order your sentences in a more unusual, thought-provoking way. Sometimes a light tone can best convey a serious message, and sometimes too colloquial a style can miss the mystery in a subject.

c)   What *sort* of poem will you write? Do some rhymes come naturally into your head? If so, it may be worth finding other rhymes too. If not – and it is more likely that rhymes won't come easily – you might be better advised to avoid rhymes altogether. The same is true of rhythms. Your starting phrases may have a natural rhythm which it would be good to repeat in the rest of the poem, either regularly or from time to time. Your poem may demand to be long and detailed, or short and punchy. Think about it.

These preliminary considerations shouldn't be sweated over. There is no point in plodding laboriously through questions like these only to miss the urge to get started, or to spend so long deciding what you intend to write that you never get around to actually writing it. Too much thought can lead to strenuous efforts to make a poem fit a chosen pattern when it is better to 'let it go'. They can be useful, however, if they are borne in mind at the outset, or if the teacher makes a point of lightly reminding the class about them when he invites his children to write.

One further preliminary: don't be intimidated by blank paper. Put something down. Good starting points are odd words, phrases, random jottings, taken directly from the child's head, not from a communal list on a board. Write these down and then fiddle with them. Throw them out or use them to trigger other ideas. Some of them may even drop complete into a poem. First thoughts needn't be correct and pure as they are noted down. Put them down as they come. Then you've got something to work on.

The elements of poetry

So far we have been considering ways in which a teacher can help with the construction of a whole poem. Now I would like to turn to some practicalities. Poetry sessions can be devoted to *practising* with words and ideas, rather than with attempts to write poems. As I said before, this is the poet's version of the sketch or doodle. Therefore it is sensible to expect no poetry to emerge from such sessions. You can never tell with creative writing, though. The silliest game can give rise to a genuine urge to write a poem. It is, however, unlikely, and we are best advised not to look for poems where none exist. The practicalities I'm talking about are rhyme, rhythm, the sound of words, the meaning, word order and imagery. Each of these can be tackled through games and exercises although it is possible to pay some attention to them at the crafting of a poem stage (see chapter 9). I shall suggest some of the games that can be used to focus attention on these things, and then I shall have something to say about dealing with them when the children are engaged in poetry writing.

Rhyme

One of the problems with rhyme in the poetry children write is that many of the rhymes are inappropriate. They are included just because they rhyme and the *meaning* of the word is ignored. This is partly because children, and adults, tend to put down the first rhyme that occurs to them. They can be encouraged to gather a selection of rhyming words and choose from it the most appropriate rhymes. Give the children a word and ask them to list as many other words as they can think of that rhyme with it in a given time – say two or three minutes. Some words lend themselves very easily to rhyme: 'night' for example. Others are more difficult and thus more challenging, even more fun: 'frost' for example. Try them with words of more than one syllable. Monty Python has come up with a poem which uses only one rhyme:

> A panto-writer, Harry Hyam
> Who was extremely fond of rhyme
> One day said to his comrades: 'I'm
> Just sick of writing pantomime
> For which I get paid half a dime,
> I'm going to write a poem sublime
> By which you'll see my fame will climb
> Above all others, for this time
> I'm only going to use ONE rhyme!'

It goes on like this for another thirty-eight lines and is, of course, more or less nonsense. It does, however, have an internal logic. An attempt has been made to link the rhymes with a rambling narrative – the rhymes dictate where the narrative goes, but it is there. Some children might enjoy this kind of challenge. How far can they get with one rhyme, whilst keeping a connecting thread through their verse?

Rhymes can come from a matching of one word with two, or with one word and part of another. In Edmond Rostand's 'Cyrano de Bergerac', the pastry cook, Ragueneau, is a devoted poet who creates this awful poem about the making of almond tarts:

> Poised on steady legs
> First your poet begs
> Several eggs.
> Froth them to mousse,
> And then introduce
> Lemon juice.
> Shimmering like silk,
> Aromatic milk
> Of almonds will c-
> ome next . . .

And so on. Children could try to create their own list of words rhymed with half words in this way.

Another way of making children more aware of rhyme is to read them a not very serious poem, like a limerick, leaving out the rhymes so that they can call them out.

> There was a young man from Dunoon
> Who always ate soup with a . . . . .
> He said 'As I eat
> Neither fish, foul nor . . . . .
> I should finish my dinner too . . . . . '

Most children will have no trouble in supplying the words 'spoon', 'meat', and 'soon'. They may, however, be surprised to learn that the words missing should really be 'fork', 'flesh' and 'quick'. This is a limerick which works because it seems to insist on certain rhymes, through a sort of poetic cloze procedure, which it then disappoints. The effect is strange to the ear, and tells us something about the power of rhyme.

Similarly, children could be given a rhyming poem and asked to change the rhymes. For example, what would happen if Matilda told not such dreadful lies but such dreaful fibs:

> Matilda told such dreadful fibs
> It startled babies in their cribs.

This can be quite a tricky exercise so it is best to try it with couplets or groups of four lines, rather than complete verses.

These suggestions, and others you can generate yourself, are aimed at getting children to play with rhyme and, thus, to become familiar with it. They should, of course, be forgotten when children have something they want to say in a poem.

Rhythm

There are two main ways of playing about with rhythm and language. One is to take the language and find the rhythm that carries it along. The other is to take a rhythm and find a language that fits it.

1. **Using the language**: take a couple of lines of poetry, or, better still in this instance, overheard snatches or phrases common to the life of the class, and say them till the rhythm is clear. Then tap out the rhythm with pencils, rulers or percussion instruments. A lot of phrases will lend themselves to more than one rhythmic interpretation. Various groups might go away and work on a collection of phrases, building up short musical pieces for percussion and then comparing them with the pieces made by other groups.

    If you take the phrase 'Alison Bartlett, are you going to be much longer?' it is possible to beat out several rhythms which fit the words.

The name, for example, could be rapped out sharply: three tripping beats followed by two solid thumps. The rest of the phrase could be done more slowly, with greater emphasis. It might be effective to allow for a dramatic pause before the last word. When this sequence has been tried and perfected, the words could be fitted back to see how they sound. Alternatively, a group might find the natural stresses in the phrase and make a jazzier rhythm out of it. To do this they need to allow a slight pause between 'you' and 'going'. If you try to fit the phrase to a steady ti-TUM ti-TUM rhythm, it doesn't work. The words make the rhythm.

2. **Using the rhythm**: take an obvious rhythm, or one picked out of a piece of music, and find some words that will fit it properly. For example, you might play the children the opening of Beethoven's 5th Symphony. The first fourteen notes provide a very strong rhythm. Is there a phrase that fits it neatly? What about:

> Porridge for tea! Porridge for tea! That's all we ever get!

or:

> Down on your knees, under the desk, make sure you don't come up!

Alternatively the words of a well-known song can be replaced by others that fit just as well:

> All things bright and beautiful,
> All creatures great and small

Could become:

> Always take your trousers off
> Before you have a bath.

The sound of words

Most words have an impact quite separate from their meaning. If you say them over and over, the meaning fades and their inner music remains. A friend of mine likes to be invited for a meal but hates the sound of the word 'meal'. Indeed, 'meal' is not a particularly attractive word. If you repeat it often enough you find your nose screwing up and your face assuming a sneer. 'Linoleum' or 'submarine', on the other hand, have a melodious ring to them. Children could compile lists of pleasant and unpleasant sounding words. Many poets have a natural ear for a musical word, or have developed a natural ear. A phrase of Eliot's from 'The Waste Land', 'murmur of maternal lamentation', I find particularly resonant. Dylan Thomas is another who seems to delight in word music. 'Fern Hill' ends like this:

> Oh as I was young and easy in the mercy of his means,
> Time held me green and dying
> Though I sang in my chains like the sea.

You can see how Thomas relishes words like 'easy', 'mercy', 'time' and 'sea'. He also adds to the musical quality of the piece by the use of alliteration: 'Mercy of his means', 'sang in my chains like the sea'. Children can create their own alliteration, not for inclusion in poems but just for the fun of making sounds. It is possible to appreciate the music of a phrase without fully understanding the meaning. The oft-quoted 'Jabberwocky' takes this a stage further by using words that have no meaning and creating a poem which sounds so marvellous that we feel it must mean something. Ask the children to write their own pieces in which made-up words feature. Because your concern is with sound rather than with rhyme or rhythm, it is probably best to ask them to write in prose – a short description of a person or an object, say. If the pieces prove particularly successful, and it seems appropriate, they can always be worked up into poems later.

Meaning

If a poem is to be true, and if its creation is to advance in some way its author's knowledge of the world, then the poem must be about something the author intends. In other words, there is little point in mastering poetic techniques in order to write about other people's ideas. Other people's ideas can spark off a child's own thoughts and enable her to write about things which have meaning for her. Too often, however, groups of children set about writing a poem called, for example, 'An Autumn Day' and incorporate plenty of their teacher's ideas.

There's something sad about this and something slightly dishonest too. For a start, it's rather unusual for a writer to come up with a title before setting about the writing. What, however, is the alternative? It's easy to imagine long, painful silences in which children are expected to come up with their own ideas and don't. Obviously, if the teacher sets a task which is too vague, like 'write a poem about something that is important to you', then he is likely to find his class floundering. There are ways of encouraging children to work with their own ideas, though. For a start, their ideas can be sought out and valued in discussion. A child may tentatively suggest a half thought-out idea. That idea can be drawn out and encouraged by questioning. Once again the teacher's role is not an easy one. He must tread a line between making no useful suggestions at all and pouncing on the comments of a child and throwing them over to the whole class for elaboration.

This is, of course, less a matter of technique than of awareness. All the same, certain techniques can be employed to increase the amount of personal involvement with a poem, to make the meaning 'truer'. One is to emphasise in questioning the *subjective* aspects of a stimulus. If, for example, you decide to take your class out for a walk as a means of starting some writing, stress that what you want to read about is not so much what the class encountered but, much more precisely, what each child saw and thought about and felt. What did you feel? The difference is only slight but is very important. It is easy for teachers to slip into a way of speaking which puts the emphasis on 'we': 'We went for a walk to the river. We thought about what it was like to be a duck.' This is often why so many class-written pieces of work sound as if they've employed an identical number of words in only a slightly varied word order. 'We' all did more or less the same. 'I' was the only one who saw things from my point of view. In writing poetry, 'I' has a better view than 'we' does.

Another technique for uncovering what the children really think or feel, is to use word association or brainstorming. Everyone starts with the same idea, or listening to the same sounds, or looking at the same images. Each child then makes a rough list of ideas, each of which has sprung from the idea that preceded it. As the list develops it becomes more personal. An example of this:

An Autumn Day

Why not? There's plenty of mileage in it as long as you don't say that the final piece of work is going to be a poem about an autumn day, entitled an autumn day.

This might conjure up a picture of dry leaves blowing across a lawn.

The idea of the leaves might lead on to a thought about how skeletal dry leaves can become.

The thought of skeletal leaves might lead to further thoughts about bones. And so on.

A final poem might take just one of these thoughts and develop that, or it might use several of the more obviously related thoughts in a considered way. The important thing is that the poem consists of ideas which mean something to the child because they were generated by the child.

Two further thoughts about using word association to trawl for ideas. In the first place, it might prove more productive to suggest that each stage is thought of as a *picture* rather than simply as a vague idea. For example, if an autumn day makes you think of sadness, don't be content with writing down the word 'sadness'. Write down words which give a brief picture of sadness – a small child alone in the corner of a playground perhaps. In the second place, the teacher should ask questions which help to make each stage vivid. It's easy for children to associate an autumn day with leaves blowing across a lawn and yet fail to register this image properly. Because it is likely that the children will be having very different thoughts, thoughts which differ more from the thoughts of their neighbour as the process goes on, the teacher cannot ask specific questions. He cannot say, for example, 'What colour are these leaves? And how many are there?' when none of the children has imagined leaves in the first place. He can, however, ask questions which bring ideas and images into sharper focus. He might start by asking, 'What picture do you see when you think of an autumn day? Is it a picture with colour in it? Do you see people in the picture? How many? Concentrate on a small part of that picture. Move into it as if you were a camera . . .' Questions like these help to make the ideas more real without tampering with them. When the teacher senses that the children are ready he can ask them to jot down a few words that will help them to recall what they've seen, and then move on to another picture, associated in some way with the first.

Accuracy is another aspect of meaning which a thoughtful teacher needs to consider in planning work for his class. Children should be encouraged not simply to say what they mean but to say *exactly* what they mean. This is no easy task these days. Much of the myth-making and story-telling which children encounter in films and on television depends for its impact on visual rather than verbal effects. Dialogue has come to play an insignificant part and has, as it were, shrunk to make way for the car chase, the helicopter crash or the blasting of a space vessel. The language that does creep into these filmed adventures is often imprecise, vague and clichéd. Only the most assured poet can make clichés sound fresh, and vagueness and imprecision are death to a poem. The teacher of poetry must, therefore, conduct a relentless battle against these things. He must become a Socratic questioner, always pressing the children to say exactly what they mean: 'A tall man? How tall? It's no good giving it in metres because that doesn't create a picture for me. Tell me something he was as tall as, or taller than. You say you felt sad? How did you feel sad? Whereabouts in your body did you feel it? Anywhere or nowhere? What did it make you do? Just sit or cry, or drum your fists?' And so on. In fact, you must come perilously close to nagging your poets. (Needless to say, your nagging must be done in the nicest possible way. You must nag to encourage, not to destroy.)

Accuracy of meaning is not the same as wordiness. The poet should search for the word or phrase that captures the precise mood or picture. Too many words can prevent the meaning from being clear. Here Wordsworth describes climbing as a boy in the Lake District:

> – Oh! when I have hung
> Above the raven's nest, by knots of grass
> And half-inch fissures in the slippery rock
> But ill-sustained, and almost, as it seem'd
> Suspended by the blast which blew amain,
> Shouldering the naked crag.
>
> William Wordsworth

The picture created in this is a vivid one. Wordsworth sets down just enough detail to make the experience seem real. If he laboured over the description of the climbing place, he would sacrifice the pace needed to suggest danger. The description would also become untrue. When you cling on for dear life what you see are the 'knots of grass' and the 'half-inch fissures'. These sum up the crag, are its most important features in this particular case.

So encourage accuracy, but also economy.

Word order

Trying out different ways of saying the same thing can bring out more interesting rhythms and place the important words in more interesting places. The children can experiment with familiar phrases or snatches drawn from various sources. For example, the sentence quoted earlier: 'Always take your trousers off before you have a bath', can be written in other ways without destroying the meaning. Most obviously:

Before you have a bath always take your trousers off.

but also:

Always, before you have a bath, take your trousers off.

or:

Take off your trousers always before you have a bath.

And so on. Each of these has a different rhythm and emphasises different words. More emphasis can be gained from repetition:

Always, always take your trousers off . . .

or:

Your trousers! Take off your trousers . . .

The children could be given a number of sentences and challenged to discover as many ways of expressing them as possible, using only the words given and repetitions. This is playing, of course, but it is playing which will help children think about word order when they come to write their own poems. It will help them to be less easily satisfied with the word order that first occurs to them and encourage them to experiment.

Imagery

I have vague memories of being taught that there were similes that were incorrect as well as similes that were correct. For example, 'as white as snow' was correct but 'as white as a beard' was not. It was permissible to say 'as white as a sheet' but only in certain circumstances. I hope this sort of thing is no longer taught because it plants in the minds of children ideas opposite to those which should be associated with the use of simile. We say things are like other things in order to make our meaning clearer, to illuminate the thing we are describing by linking it with some other thing:

My love is like a red, red rose . . .

This tells us something about my love: not that she has green leaves and thorns and needs watering. Imagery is a two-way process. In this case we accept aspects of the rose which chime with aspects of my love, and ignore the rest. The more ideas chime with each other the more powerful the imagery will prove. Children can be encouraged to find chiming images all around them: people who are like animals, or buildings or plants, feelings that are like objects, or sounds or colours. They should not be made to feel that there is only one correct comparison to be made ('the dress was as white as snow'), but should be invited to experiment ('the dress was as white as a swan's back'). Once they've experimented, they can find the image which chimes the most. The idea of a swan's back, for example, may chime more with a dress, the way it moves etc., than snow does. An image which produces many harmonies, rather than a single chime, can be extended to take an even greater part in a poem. Thus 'The sea is a hungry dog' works at several levels. It paints a picture of a dog and of the sea as if it were a dog. It tells us something more about both a dog and the sea which we wouldn't have known without the comparison. Here is the first verse:

> The sea is a hungry dog,
> Giant and grey.
> He rolls on the beach all day.
> With his clashing teeth and shaggy jaws
> Hour upon hour he gnaws
> The rumbling, tumbling stones,
> And, 'Bones, bones, bones, bones!'
> The giant sea-dog moans,
> Licking his greasy paws.
>
> *James Reeves*

Children can make both sorts of comparison: the short one which focuses on detail ('a hand like twigs', 'he ran like a deer') and the extended one which develops a comparison at length. As they become used to making comparisons, to collecting lists of them, for example, they can begin to drop the use of words like 'as' or 'like'. Thus 'his eyes were currants in a wedge of lifeless suet' can have more impact than 'his eyes were *like* currants ...' Children can be alerted to look out for places where the imagery can be made more direct. Sessions in which they generate as many and as far-reaching a collection of images as possible can be rewarding. They can order the images they collect placing the most appropriate ones, those which chime the most, first and discarding those that don't work hard enough or which chime in the wrong kind of way.

Tackling a poem

How do you help children with technique when the exercises are set aside and the class is engaged in poetry writing proper? To be frank, there isn't a lot you can do which won't threaten a child's personal involvement with her work. As we have said elsewhere, you have to tread a careful line between advising and interfering. Therefore, at the writing stage you have to do more trusting than tinkering.

(a) You have to trust that the diet of poetry you have provided is doing its subtle work: influencing, though not to the extent of inviting imitations.
(b) You have to trust to the groundwork you have already done: the word games and the exercises in looking and thinking etc. You won't want to bring them too much to the fore by, for example, calling out to the quietly working children, 'Don't forget all that stuff we did on imagery the other week!' This may mean that the 'imagery stuff' gets into the poem and the poetry itself is squeezed out.
(c) You have to trust to your own relationship with your children: that they know you take poetry writing seriously, that they feel at liberty to write what they want without inhibition. In other words you have to trust that they trust you.
(d) Above all, you must trust the children themselves: believe that they have something to say and a voice with which to say it.

It sounds as if all you need to is stand back and let the poetry take place but, of course, it isn't as simple as that. All this trusting cannot happen without a lot of effort and real enthusiasm on your part. It must be prepared for, and the preparation is what this book is about.

There is something else you can do. Assuming that your children are becoming familiar with the techniques of drafting and editing, you can guide their work by careful questioning (see chapter 8). This really means you must hold consultations with individual children. No doubt there will be certain points you can address to groups of children, but your most effective work will probably be done in conversations with each child. This makes two important and heavy demands on you as a teacher. You must make time to talk to the children and you must ensure that, when you do talk, both you and the children understand your role. Finding time may be the hardest thing you do and you'll probably have to compromise. If you're well organised you'll make sure that children who missed the opportunity to chat about their work whilst engaged on one poem, will be seen the next time. Your role in these consultations is not that of the poetry expert, the one who has the answers and can lick a rough poem into better shape. The children should learn to regard you as someone whose opinion may prove helpful, someone who can *suggest* ways of improving their work. Equally, they should see you are someone with whom they can disagree. Ultimately, the decisions about what is or isn't changed in a poem must remain the poet's, that is to say the children write their poems and the teacher sees how he can help without leaving his mark on the work.

A teacher's desire to be involved in acts of creativity should be directed towards his own writing. Children will be quicker to appreciate the value of writing if they know their teacher writes as well. Of course, it is likely that much of his time at school will be taken up with his responsibility to the children, but there is no reason why a teacher should not make some sort of attempt at writing with his class. (If he is genuinely involved in what he writes he will want to finish it in his own time.) He can judge for himself whether or not to read out to them what he has written.

Those who find writing difficult

It is all too easy to become confused about the aims of the poetry session. It can seem that the aim is to encourage 'good' English (that is to say acceptable, consistent, accurate English), and yet, if you become too concerned about how 'good' the English is, you can deprive a piece of its integrity and vigour. It can even seem that spelling, punctuation and handwriting are part of the poetry session. These are understandable assumptions but they are wrong. Poetry sessions are about ideas and the language that carries them. Poems are only written down so that we can communicate with those not present and remember our own ideas. Poems can be made up and worked on in a child's head. They can go straight onto a tape recorder (see chapter 8). We tend to write poems down because it is the most efficient way of dealing with them, not because it is the only way. Therefore, poetry is as valuable an activity for those who find writing difficult as it is for everyone else, and there are a number of things we can do to encourage them in it.

1. Emphasise that the thing which counts is the poem and not its written representation. You want the child's own ideas more than you want a string of fancy words. Ideas come from the head and are floating about all the time.
2. A poem needn't be long. It can be short enough to be memorised.
3. The teacher, or someone else, can write down the ideas for the child who finds writing difficult. A lot can be achieved in a time of consultation in this case (see chapter 8).
4. Use tape recorders. Children who can scarcely write a word can record poems of epic proportions which range over all sorts of subjects in vivid fashion. It doesn't really matter who takes on the job of committing it all to the written word, except, of course, in terms of the time and energy busy teachers have available for such work.

Guard against the assumption that the child who finds writing difficult can only be a poorer kind of poet. It's simply untrue. If children who are labelled 'under-achievers' don't make good poems, it's often because no one expects them to!

'This is just to say'
(William Carlos Williams)

8 Responding to children's poetry

This chapter attempts to deal with the following issues:
- the importance of sensitive handling of the poetry children write
- responding to children's poetry rather than'marking'
- different phases in replying to children's writing
- helping the less able writer
- some examples of children's poems with the teacher's written response

The importance of sensitive handling

The way a child's poem is received and responded to by her teacher may be the most significant factor in that child's development as a writer. Sooner or later in poetry, a young writer will say something personal and important about her life and the way she feels; these might be thoughts she has not shared with anyone before. Alternatively, she might not even be aware she has expressed something revealing about herself. To respond to such poetry requires great sensitivity on the part of the teacher. If the child's poetry is casually received it will be some time, if ever, before she will risk revealing herself again. We have to be tactful, delicate and reassuring with the young writers in our care.

Even if the poem is not particularly deep or serious, the writer takes risks in putting pen to paper and is anxious about the reactions of the reader. Although there can and should be a variety of 'audiences' for a child's poem, the reality is that for most of the time the teacher is the principal reader. Clearly if a teacher replies to a child's poem with harshness or insensitivity that child is likely to stick to safe and predictable writing in the future. Most teachers, as caring professionals, will not respond in an unkind or thoughtless way. But how often are we too busy to read a poem eagerly thrust before us? Do we always take the time to read each child's offering carefully and responsively? Are we always aware of letting the child flushed with the success of her poem have the opportunity of reading it out to the group? Do we keep in our minds during a writing session the sheer hard work that goes into it, the efforts each individual has made? Of course we are only human, but in so far as we fail, what messages do the children receive about the way we view their poetry?

And what about the light-hearted poetry children engage in? Do we have to be equally careful with that? I think we do. This was brought home to me by my own son who, although gifted with words, is not particularly keen on writing. One morning before school he very uncharacteristically wrote a limerick. He bounded through to my bedroom and read it eagerly. I have never much cared for limericks so I listened to his less than brilliant composition, my mind on other things. I started to say 'Very nice, love' when I noticed his face. I realised then that this piece of nonsense verse mattered to him and that my response was important. I made an effort to read the limerick and respond to it properly. Later in the day he memorised it, and repeated it to his father with gusto.

This moment of awareness has been significant in my own teaching. On several occasions I have stopped myself from reacting casually and without due thought to humorous pieces by young writers. I've been about to brush them aside with a smile and pleasantry, ready to immerse myself in weightier things, busy and distracted as teachers often are. I hope I have always caught myself in time, because I have seen that look on other children's faces. 'It may be funny, even silly, but it's my writing – don't dismiss it.'

Those of you who have actually tried writing will know what hard work it is, how sensitive one is to criticism, how afraid to put one's own words down on the page and be judged by them. Donald Graves aptly says that if you are going to be a writer you have to be prepared to be a public nudist! Any writing of value reveals much about the writer. Young children may be less self conscious, but they are just as sensitive as adults. And don't we provide good models to our classes, if we teachers occasionally sit down with the children and compose and share our writing alongside them? Student teachers have remarked to me that it was writing with the children that taught them most about the writing process. Others have said that sharing writing in this way made a tremendous impact on their pupils' attitudes to it.

The teacher walks a minefield in responding to children's poetry. He has to boost the confidence of his young writers, who know that their writing rarely matches the lively ideas they had at the outset. He has to encourage the natural diffidence of anyone who has reached the age of self-awareness (around eight), when a piece of her writing has to be shared. And he has to contend with the fact that, in this personal mode of writing, any criticism of the poem can be taken for a criticism of the writer herself.

And I have not touched yet on the notion of improvement. How do we help young writers to develop in poetry? What sort of errors should we point out? What advice should we offer? Do we have to understand the technicalities of poetry ourselves first? Some of these issues will be addressed later in the chapter (others are considered in chapters 7 and 9).

Responding to children's poetry rather than 'marking'

You will note that the term 'marking' has not been used so far. Some explanation for the rejection of this term is required. It is totally inappropriate to 'mark' a poem. No teacher would dream of scrawling over a child's painting – we accept these works of art, and display them *all* on the wall, gifted or not. Teachers might make suggestions while children paint and create, and, on occasion dab in the odd section to teach a point. But they never blot out parts of the painting or construction or tell the child that bits of it are 'wrong'.

Yet with children's poetry, no less a creative activity, we sometimes think it is permissible to score words out in red, put marks all over the text and a comment underneath. Many children feel resentful about this – they have told me so. Try asking your own class. They feel that their writing is part of themselves, it was hard work to construct and they resent it being defaced, even by the best-intentioned teacher.

There are several ways of getting round this problem. First of all, if children learn to draft, then a teacher's comment on a rough text will be similar to what the writer is attempting herself (see chapter 9). However, if children are expected to engage in writing only once and reach the finished product in one sitting, then at the very least the teacher can make comments in pencil which can be rubbed out later. Alternatively, a comment can be pinned to the text and later removed.

Most importantly we must strive to get away from a 'marking' mentality, where we focus on errors rather than achievement. If a piece of work that meant something to a writer is returned covered in red ink or with some bland, largely meaningless comment like 'good', 'try harder', 'watch your spelling', that writer may see little point of making a great effort in the future. I don't mean to suggest that children consciously think things out in this way, but it will be the end result just the same. Would you feel like showing a piece of personal writing to someone who might glance at it superficially to highlight mistakes and did not make constructive comments?

So how do we go about it? We can begin by making a genuine *reply* to what the poem had to say. The comments could be of this variety:

'I liked ...'
'I enjoyed the ...'
'I felt ...'
'I wondered if ...'
'It made me think of ...'

And before any assessment of the poem's worth is made, the pupil can be given encouragement. There is always something positive you can say to a pupil who has worked hard:

'That's lovely, you have written a lot ...'

'You have tried very hard with that poem – well done ...'
'I can see you enjoyed writing this ...'
'I know it was hard work. I am very pleased with you ...'
The pupil whose work is returned with a warm comment, sees it attractively displayed or put in the class anthology, is likely to try harder next time, striving to improve.

Of course, false praise is not useful. There is no point in telling a child her poem is good, if it clearly does not make sense, or that her work has improved if it has not. But the comments indicated above are not untruthful, though they are tactful. One can make a positive response in this way, with some gentle suggestion for improvement, without fulsome praise that is not true. Children sense such insincerity a mile off.

Different phases in replying to children's poetry

Let's look now at some possible phases in replying to children's poetry:
instant oral
considered written
group appreciation

Instant oral response by the teacher

When the children settle down to write, take the opportunity to get round the class or group, offering instant feedback. This is also a good time to help children with writing problems which I deal with later in the chapter. You can react to the pupil's opening lines, finding something to praise. This encouragement can give an impetus to further effort. Hearing her first couple of lines read aloud appreciatively can give a tremendous boost to the writer. However, it is as well to remember that some pupils like to get on without disturbance and would find such teacher behaviour intrusive. It is part of being respectful of our pupils that we try to be aware of their different writing strategies.

As children write at different speeds, in a class poetry writing session some children finish before others and want to show their poems to their teacher. This tends to happen at a busy part of the 'lesson', when the teacher may be helping a less confident writer to compose. It takes a lot of skill to cater for the varying needs and demands of a class at different stages of the writing process.

Here are some practical points:

- Get the organisation as streamlined as possible: don't waste valuable time in classroom management issues like what a child does next, which book to write in, etc. These issues should be sorted out in advance.
- Be aware of your priorities in a writing session and stick to them: e.g. struggling writers first, those needing help next, finally those who have finished.

- Children should have something quiet and relatively undemanding to get on with when they have finished their poems and are waiting for your attention.
- Children should be taught not to interrupt the teacher when he is working with another pupil.
- Teachers can learn to skim finished poems for two main purposes: to reply positively to the poem itself, stressing one or two successful features; to see whether there is work to be done on the poem right away, time permitting.
  Is the poem unfinished?
  Could it be longer?
  Should it be cut?
  Is there a word, phrase or line which needs attention?
  Is there a section which could be easily improved?
  Is the poem ready to be rewritten neatly for the pupil's own anthology, for display? In this case the teacher might draw the pupil's attention to aspects of spelling, punctuation, structure suitable to her age and ability

These oral comments are important to the pupil whose poem is still 'warm' and fresh. She will read your remarks with interest when her poem is returned, but the spontaneity is lost, the poem is a little stale by then.

Considered written response by the teacher

The written comments you make on a poem will be the pupil's only record of your opinion. Often elaboration is required in a short discussion with the pupils when the work is handed back; others will need to have the comments read to them. Clearly this takes time and has to be built into the organisation of classroom life, but things that are important do take time.

It seems to me that there are four main strands in our written responses to pupils' poems:

1. Reply to what the poem had to say, to the spirit of the poem.
2. Indicate what were the strengths of the poem.
3. Offer advice for improvement if appropriate – you can only expect a pupil to cope with one or two points at a sitting.
4. You may want to make a suggestion for further writing or reading.
   Examples of this approach are shown later in the chapter.

In developing the notion of encouragement and sincerity in dealing with children's poetry, let us consider for a moment the second point above – namely, telling a child what was *successful* in her writing. Most of us find it pretty easy to pick out mistakes and weaknesses in writing. But how often do we demonstrate to children what is good in their work? The point is that children do not necessarily know what is successful unless we tell them. A child may be pleased to see an encouraging comment in her book, but she may have little comprehension what it was about her work that pleased her teacher today yet disappointed him yesterday. A teacher who makes *specific comments* about effective features in a poem, gives that child a sense of what to aim for in the future.

Perhaps this is dangerous ground for those of you reading this book who are not experienced teachers of poetry. Perhaps you feel hesitant about making direct comments to children because you are not sure you know what makes a poem successful: the technical terms, why the language was effective, etc. Let me reassure you that this feeling of inadequacy is shared by all of us who have embarked on this field, and is common among teachers trying out a new area of the curriculum or a new approach. You will become more confident of your ability to assess poetry the more of it you do and the more of it you read. The latter is important. Poetry itself will teach you about poetry. And remember that no two teachers (or poets or critics) would necessarily agree about what constitutes a good poem, in the same way that no two people would react in the same way to a given poem. It is a very personal and idiosyncratic thing.

But if you spend time with a child sharing your response to her poem, telling her what you enjoyed about it, this is likely to be beneficial to the child as a writer, however undeveloped your poetic discrimination. After all, you are unlikely to praise weak features in her writing. You may lack confidence in yourself at first, but there is no better measure than your intuitive judgement. And you can read more poetry yourself, attend in-service courses to help your own development. The child will have another teacher next year who may look for different things in poetry, so she will receive a balance of viewpoints in her school career (if she is lucky enough to encounter teachers who give poetry a significant place in the curriculum). There are no generally accepted criteria about what makes a good poem, though most of us can recognise one when we see it. Have confidence in your intuitive response to the child's poem, be open to what the child has to offer rather than looking for a particular style that appeals to you, be discriminating too – don't be prepared to accept mediocre work as the norm; most importantly, try to suspend your 'correction' or 'marking' mentality which all of us in this profession share to some extent, in favour of a genuine response and you will probably make a good job of it.

The business of helping pupils to improve their *own* poetry is a controversial one. Some teachers believe that a child's poetry is beyond criticism and should be simply accepted and appreciated. I have some sympathy with this view, but as teachers it is our job to seek to develop the child's ability to write. The suggestions we make can be sensitive, constructive and tempered by praise, as I have already indicated. If our policy can be one of intervention without inference, we can nurture the developing artist in the child and help to develop her skill at the same time.

When I suggest that children might try to improve their writing with the help of their teachers, I do not mean that teachers ought to alter the pupil's work in any direct way, supply alternative words, etc. That would be interference. What we want to do is to help children draw on their considerable latent store of vocabulary and knowledge of language. By contact with adults and each other, television and advertising, children have a fund of language experience which we have to encourage them to tap.

Be wary of asking for 'good' vocabulary. What are 'good' words in the context of a poem? It is surely *how* the words are used that counts, how they fit together for effect. Some teachers encourage the use of adjectives. This is equally dubious. Very little good poetry features an abundance of adjectives; in fact they often detract from rather than improve a piece of writing. A quick look at the work of a popular poet like Ted Hughes is enough to confirm both points.

So how can we help children to improve their own poetry? Unintentional errors can be pointed out, advice given on the structure of a poem, suggestions made for where poems might be elaborated or cut. The use of sloppy language can be queried; e.g. 'nice', 'pretty', 'beautiful' ... words which do not convey much impact and are generalisations. Clichés and flowery, exaggerated or melodramatic language can be questioned. I don't pretend that this is not a challenging exercise, particularly at first, but it does get easier with experience.

Group appreciation

It is imperative that we make time to read out children's own poetry. Whenever possible this should happen straight after the writing session, but better later in the week than never. Those of you who feel there isn't time to read out poems as well as write them in a poetry session should consider expanding the time available: perhaps an hour and a half first thing in the morning, and see if the results are an improvement. When I plan a poetry session with children, I divide my time roughly into three parts:

⅓− introduction and stimulus

⅓+ writing

⅓ reading out

In the ideal set-up the pupils sit round in a semi-circle, everybody close to each other and to the teacher, a friendly group. As many children as can be fitted in read out their poems which should get a second reading by the teacher (it is hard to take in a poem after only one hearing.) The teacher's reading is likely to be the only chance the pupil will get to hear her poem read aloud well. A sensitive reading will highlight all the possibilities in the poem and present it in the most favourable light. As well as reading the poems, we can encourage pupils to make positive comments on each other's poetry.

- What did you particularly like about that poem?
- Was there a word or phrase you thought was skilfully used?
- What was the best bit for you?
- Why did you enjoy the poem?

With the right atmosphere the children will soon make this part of the session their own, although it can take some weeks to reach a mature and discriminating level of discussion. The teacher must give a lead here, finding the right moment to delve more deeply, bringing in new ideas when the children get into a rut. We can do most good if we concentrate on the success in each child's work. Young children are not ready for public criticism (are we ever ready?) In fact, children are generous to one another in these sessions if the teacher sets the right tone. It should not be competitive. Children tend to be supportive of the less able members of the group. It will not be long before the children become perceptive and thoughtful in their remarks, often noticing aspects of poetry the teacher has failed to see. Unkind contributions should be disallowed from the outset, and children soon learn what is acceptable. I have been working in this way for fifteen years, and I can honestly say I have never encountered a mean comment, though in other situations I am well aware that children are often unpleasant to one another!

This is also a wonderful opportunity to teach aspects of technique which come up naturally and meaningfully. You can tell the class that such and such in Joe's poem is a simile, and ask them to look out for others. You can show them the form Katie adopted for her poem, how it affects the way the poem is read out and, indeed, what it means. You can talk about imagery used by pupils: words, phrases, lines that evoke a picture. You can point out different usage of rhythm, repetition, rhyme . . . The possibilities are endless. So the reading out and discussion is both a time of learning and sharing and is generally very popular with children who have a marvellous capacity to listen for longish periods of time, as well as participate in this set up.

Children who find it hard to write

Most children who find it difficult to write poetry find the act of writing difficult as well. We need to offer these children generalised help in tackling writing which it is not my brief to explore in this book. But let us focus for a moment on less able writers. Can we help them to write successful poetry?

The answer is yes – we can do a great deal for them through the medium of poetry. A poem is a very accessible form of writing for younger and less able children. It is much less demanding than narrative, the most popular mode of writing in junior schools. A poem can begin where the writer is: 'I saw', 'I felt', 'I like', so she can get straight in. This is the part of writing most children find difficult – getting to where the action is. There need be no hard and fast rules like sentence structure and punctuation as in prose (at least until a later stage) so the child is able to experiment and play with language. And if a short poem is what is asked for, the child is far more likely to manage something successful. And we all know how important success and motivation are to struggling writers.

Often I act as scribe for my writers. I ask the child to tell me what she wants to say. If nothing is forthcoming, I suggest she closes her eyes and imagines. Sometimes a poem, picture, object relating to the theme can be read or looked at again. If the child is still wary, I ask her to tell me what she sees, hears, thinks in her head in her own words. I remind her that everyone has something unique to say in a poem that is worth hearing; it is a question of being quiet and listening to ourselves. Sometimes it takes time and doesn't come easily. I have never yet drawn a blank – something comes out, and I 'shape' it into the first couple of lines of a poem (see chapter 4).

I then read the lines back to the child, perhaps a few times, encouraging her to say more. On occasion a direct question or two are necessary. I then read it all back appreciatively and ask the child to compose the last line(s) herself. This rarely fails, though at first many children don't have the confidence to manage much themselves. It may take weeks for this confidence to develop.

Otherwise the most common problem children experience in writing poetry relates to form. This will automatically improve as children gain more experience of reading, hearing and writing their own poetry. Our aims should be long-term; we cannot expect our pupils to master such complexities in a brief period of time.

Giving our pupils a simple form in which to write can be liberating. Taking a new line at a natural pause can also be a breakthrough to 'free verse'. Again it may take the less able writer some weeks to master even this shape. The teacher needs to work with the pupil both at the time of composition and later when the poem has been written. The authors of this book have experienced every kind of difficulty in their time. Poetry does come eventually for almost every type of child we encounter. Belief in the child's ultimate success, of having something worth saying and the means to say it, even at the time of greatest struggle, is vital.

Experimenting with poetry

Once a child can manage 'free verse' I encourage experimentation. Poetry is a most adaptable mode of language and it offers opportunities for children to manipulate words so that they work *for* rather than against the writer. I want to help young writers find out what words can do and what they can do with words. Here are some examples:

The Creation
Dark, shapeless
   Endless, empty
   Deserted, barren
Wind-swept
      dead
was the world before Creation.

The mighty one
    GOD
Looked down with his powerful eyes ...   *Harriet 9*

Harriet was encouraged to play around with where the words went on the page. As well as weaving her own version out of the dramatic language of the Bible, she uses the original device of starting with eight adjectives followed by a verb. Such experimentation by a child so young is extremely unlikely in any other mode of writing.

Old Tree

O! I wither away
O! Lord
I'm not old lord
not old
yet I die.
My boughs grow weary
but I'm not old lord
two hundred years or so
not old
not old lord.

Alex 9

Here Alex writes a song-like poem with a refrain; he uses repetition most effectively.

The Rotting Bridge

The flycatcher and buntings chirp around me,
The stream of reeds glisten.
Ahead the bridge of iron and wood stands silently.
Over the bridge is a ditch,
In the ditch are some reeds,
In the reeds a sedge warbler hops. How close can I get?
The rotting sleepers on the iron rails
Wait for me.
Cautiously I cross.

Daniel 10

In the middle of this wonderfully evocative piece of writing, packed with detailed observation, Daniel uses a familiar poetic technique:

Over the bridge is a ditch,
In the ditch are some reeds,
In the reeds a . . .

There's Eight of Them

There's eight of them.
What – eight of them?
Yes, eight of them I said.
There's three water lilies down below
And two robins up ahead
That will make thirteen they said.

There's eight of them.
What – eight of them?
Yes, eight of them I said.
There's water down below
And the moon up ahead.
That will make ten
That's what I said.

Lisa 10

Lisa employs a different kind of repetition in a poem inspired by an Arthur Rackham illustration of dwarf-like creatures crossing a river by some water-lilies. I had asked the children to look at their pictures from an unexpected angle. Lisa certainly does so, and her rhythmic refrain adds greatly to this mysterious little poem.

Some examples of children's poems with the teacher's written response

To illustrate some of the points I have been making, I have chosen some poems written for me by different children with the comments I wrote to them at the time. I do not wish to set myself up as any model of excellence and know that I fall well short of the ideal. But readers might find it helpful to see a possible response to the chosen poems, even if they disagree with my conclusions.

The first two poems were by first year juniors both of whom were struggling with writing at this stage and neither of whom were high fliers.

A Dreamy Poem

Ballet is dreamy water
the flowers coming out
slowly at first
dancing at a palace
and some very graceful music.

age 8

This was the best piece of writing this child had done all year. It was full of spelling mistakes and the handwriting was very difficult to read. What could I say to show this child my appreciation of her effort?

'I enjoyed your poem very much. It made me think about a fairy tale world with princes and princesses. It made me feel very dreamy, as I floated along with your words. I liked the way you said that ballet *is* dreamy water. That's a good thing to do in poetry – to suggest that something can also be something else. I liked the idea of the flowers coming out "slowly" at first. What if you had put slowly in a line on its own? I would really have had to stop and read it.

Most of all I think this is a good poem because you managed to take me to where you went in your imagination.

Write this out again beautifully to put in our special book of poems. Have a try with the words that I have underlined (spelling). We can work on them together if you need help.'

This child's work went from strength to strength. (I don't manage a comment as long as this for every child and every piece of writing. And an eight-year-old backward reader obviously needed to have the comments read to her. But I think it is important to write them just the same.)

The next poem was by a child who was slower than the first and rather unhappy at the time.

Butterflies

Long thin beginning to be patterned
then she flutters her wings
and she was gay she flies and flies
O why does she not come to me
come *come* to me o please *please*
come to me kind come to me
then she turns up she speeds
then down she comes again

age 8

'What a lovely poem! I could just imagine the gorgeous butterfly that you seemed to be watching in your poem. How carefully you watched it and what a lot of things you noticed about it. Because you did that so well, I can almost see that butterfly too. I think you really liked that butterfly and would have liked to have it for yourself. But it flew away in the end, as wild things do. I particularly enjoyed your opening two lines and your last line. Read them again and see if you like them too.

You have repeated some words in your poem. This can be a good thing to do in a poem, because you really look closely at a word that has been repeated. Did you intend to repeat the words I have underlined? Sometimes we do it by mistake. Read it again and see what you prefer.

You have worked really well today. I wonder what you will write next?'

With older and more experienced pupils, one can be more searching in response to their poetry. The two examples that follow are by gifted and keen writers who both attended Poetry Club for some years. (Poetry Club is a workshop I ran for six years on Saturday mornings for local school children. Some of the children stayed on for years. All chose to come themselves.)

The first was by a girl who could always produce a good poem, whatever the subject suggested. However, her writing had become rather stale and contrived. She had got into the habit of using self-conscious, pseudo-poetic language; her poems lacked authenticity and she certainly needed a challenge. But, of course, I did not want to hurt her feelings or dampen her enthusiasm. And it must also be remembered that most adolescents go through a period where their writing is very much influenced by what they read; it tends to 'go off' for a time and this seems to be an inescapable phase before the more mature style develops.

Hinges

A source for unlimited stimuli,
The entrance to eternity; Open.

A block, toppling hope in one blow.
A dead end, finality; Shut.

The lock slides into place, closing me off,
Providing a welcome escape from the outside world.

A room would not be full without a door.

age 9

'A thoughtful poem with a brilliant last line. It's the sort of line I wish I could have written. It just seems right. Overall a strong and effective poem, and a very melancholy one. Your mastery of punctuation is very good.

A few points: I like the contrast between the closed and open doors in the first two verses, but I sense you are striving hard for effect. For example, I wasn't sure about "unlimited stimuli", "entrance to eternity". Are they really your words? What do you mean? Look at them again and see what you think.

Does "welcome" in line 6 add anything to the meaning? The simplicity of the last line is something you might try to work on. The title is perfect.

Vasco Popa wrote some marvellous poems about things like doors and windows. I'll bring them next week.'

My questions to this girl are real ones. She is much more talented at creative writing than I am. I am not sure that I know the answers better than her. But it is important for her development that I try to extend her.

The last poem is by a boy who was at his first session of Poetry Club. I could tell that this was a child for whom words flowed fluently and easily. I could also tell that he thought that poetry had to be refined, and was giving me the sort of poem children often think that teachers want. In the coming weeks I encouraged him to play with language and bring his sense of humour into his poetry.

Five Ways of Looking at the Sea

Mountainous black waves combing a blue-black surface
               (first attempt: an endless void)
Infinite and endless attacks against the rocks whipping them
with spray.

Calm and peaceful the sea lies dormant
untouched by any mood or vice.

Serenely the waves sway, unmarked apart from shoals
of silver as fishes dart beneath.

Covering as a blanket, holding as a great hand
the sea clutches at the wonders of the sea-bed.

age 10

'A very fine first poem. I can see I am going to enjoy working with you! I liked a lot of things about this poem: the contrast in moods you convey, the use of particular words – "whipping", "dark", "clutches", your attention to detail, your ability to use words dramatically. But most of all I admire your last verse which is superb: "covering as a blanket, holding as a great hand" … lovely.

There are one or two things you might like to look at. Do you remember I asked you if you could improve on "endless void"? I explained that other people had used that expression before and I wanted you to find your own words. I wonder about "blue-black"? Are you happy with it? Could you work on this line?

Once or twice I feel uncertain about the words you use. Will you look at them again and decide whether they really convey what you want to say – "infinite", "endless", "dormant", "vice". These are all interesting words, but are they the best words to use in this poem? You make your own mind up.

I can't wait to see what you write next …'

Two years later, by then a secondary pupil, he was writing with confidence, sophistication and simplicity.

A poem is an iron bar
That I must bend into a
          beautiful thing
With the hammer and anvil
          of my mind.
The hotter my furnace, the
          easier it is.

A poem is a tunnel one
          must dig with a teaspoon.

I have just written a poem
    about as comfortable as a
          richocheting laser beam.

A poet is he who is always
    groping for that which is just
          out of reach.

A poet is he who pleads
'For God's sake, don't go now –
          hear me out!'

A poet is he who rides wild horses
Holds bubbles,
And steps unhurt from roaring fires.

A poet is he who says
'Come a hair-breadth closer,
and I will reveal my
innermost feelings.'

A poet is he who splices frayed
          tempers
Calms troubled waters,
And dilutes rage.

Jonathan 12

The way I work with children on their poetry is more like a collaborator, I
hope, than a teacher, in a workshop rather than a lesson. Certainly I am more
experienced at reading and thinking about poetry, and I am more know-
ledgeable about how poetry works. But in making decisions about what do
do with a poem, I am not necessarily more skilled than the child who wrote it.
In some ways I am definitely less so. The child knows what her intentions
were. Although I am always advocating experimentation in poetry, I have
caught myself 'correcting' inventive use of language because it did not
conform to my expectations. Fortunately I have encountered children who
said 'No, I meant it like that' and have felt suitably chastened! Even if I am
pretty sure my advice is sound, I would never seek to impose my opinion

on a pupil. It must be up to the pupil to reject or accept our suggestions, if they are to be the owners of their own writing.

It is vital that we are prepared to accept our pupils' judgement of their own writing. If we do this, they will be prepared to take it seriously and make sensible decisions about it, though we will not always agree with them. We can offer enlightened feedback, but ultimately the pupil should take responsibility for her own writing.

Probably the most significant attitude we need to convey to our pupils is respect for their endeavours. Once I asked the twenty or so children waiting for Poetry Club to start on a lovely sunny day why they came. Why didn't they go out and enjoy all the things children like doing on hot Saturday mornings? They offered a variety of reasons, but by far the most popular was something to the effect that 'we do better work here'. The children came to do a job of work, for the satisfaction of creating a successful poem.

Michael Armstrong, in his insightful *Closely Observed Children*, reminds us of 'the careful, yet uncertain skill with which children express their ideas in the appropriate literary form with *very serious purpose*' (my emphasis). Likewise, Norman MacCaig, the Scottish poet, writing an introduction to a book of poetry by children had this to say:

> If it is characteristic of a poet to write his own rich experience, to think in unexpected and elliptical ways, to create remarkable images and live on such close terms with his own language that he can play the fool with it when he chooses to, then the creators of many of these verses are poets – little ones, without much stamina and easily silenced.

It is the last two phrases we must take on board as teachers. Our encouragement, sensitivity and understanding are necessary to sustain the stamina of young writers and make sure they are not easily silenced.

9 Drafting and editing

Most good poems are created through a process of drafting and editing. Too often, however, we are tempted to concentrate less on this stage than on the finished product. We become interested in something we can see or assess and we tend to ignore the importance of what goes on inside the writer. Sometimes our interest in a final product yields little more than display fodder – pieces which may look good but which have been produced with little real involvement on the part of the child.

Bearing this in mind, it is a good idea to teach children that poems do not, on the whole, drop ready-made from heaven. Between the glimmering of the first idea and the final product a lot of work has to take place, much of it in the form of drafting and editing. However, it is not enough simply to *tell* children that a lot of work is required. The word 'work' is charged with meaning which is not altogether pleasant for some children. Therefore, rather than replace the notion of poems dropping ready-made from heaven with that of poems hewn out of rock by sweated labour, it is probably better to provide children with some strategies. These are strategies to help them move from the appearance of an idea in their minds to the poem in its final state. The ideas for drafting and editing which I discuss here refer largely to children of nine and over (see chapter 3).

What follows is an annotated list of some stages which might be employed in the drafting and editing of a poem.

1. **The idea**: note down odd words or phrases as they come to mind. Some people find these easier to scatter round the page at random. Others may feel more at ease if they put them into some kind of order, even if it's no more than one idea on a new line beneath the one before. It really doesn't matter. It's unlikely that anyone will see it at this stage.

   The implications for the teacher are fairly obvious. He must provide the physical means – scrap-paper or personal notebooks over which the children know he will not be casting a pedantic eye. He must also provide the time for this stage to produce real ideas in the children, and he must avoid giving them his own ideas to be reworked and returned to him in a different form.

2. **The first draft**: this is likely to consist of words and phrases from the first stage strung together to make more sense. Some of the early ideas will be rejected and others will be developed. It is an important stage: the discovery of pattern in random (or apparently random) jottings. It is still, however, rough and ready. If the poem is to be a long one the first draft may even be in prose.

3. **Tinkering with the first draft**: I avoid the word 'correcting' because it implies that the writer must get rid of things in the first draft because they are wrong. This need not be the case. Ideas, words, images can be taken out at this stage and put back later on. So this is tinkering rather than correcting, and it is likely that it will concern four elements:
   a) Things to cut – especially if parts of the poem have started out as prose, certain words and even some phrases will be superfluous. Encourage economy. Discourage opulent indulgence and attempts to 'sound' poetic – 'maggot ostentation' as Shakespeare called it.
   b) The language – could some of the original words be replaced by better ones? Better sounding? More accurate? The answer to these questions is almost always yes. Of course, the children must find their *own* replacements. Better must be better for *them*, as they see things.
   c) The word order – could some bits be effectively repeated? Could some important words be given more prominence by placing them nearer the end or the beginning of lines? Do you need to reconsider the length of the lines?
   d) Rhythm and rhyme – even in so-called free verse certain words can be made more effective if they chime with other words. Similarly, a phrase or a line can work better if a little tinkering retains the sense while stressing the rhythm.

4. **The second draft**: make a fair copy of what you've got so far, without the crossings out and the arrows and overscribbling which are an essential part of stage three. Read what you've got. Are you still writing the poem you intended to write, or has your intention changed? It doesn't matter if it has changed but it's useful to know. Compare this draft with the first draft and even with the ideas stage. Can it be improved by including things from those earlier attempts? Or, indeed, do those earlier attempts work better anyway?

5. **Repeat stages three and four**: of course, this may not be necessary. One of the things a child must learn about these processes is when to *stop* tinkering. It can be tempting to tinker on until all freshness has been driven out of a poem.

6. **The proving**: if it is at all possible – and I can't think of many reasons why, with planning, it shouldn't be – put the poem away for a while. Come back to it after a couple of days, or a week perhaps, and try to look at it with a fresh eye. If you're lucky, nothing will need changing. Otherwise you will be better placed to spot those bits that don't quite

look or sound right. During this time of waiting the poem proves, like bread waiting to be baked. Needless to say, the writing – the marks on the paper – don't change at all but those marks are not really the poem. They merely represent the poem which, in reality, remains in your head.

There should really be two proving times: one between the idea and the writing (see chapter 3) and one between the penultimate draft and the final version.

Each of these stages – and any of the other stages that you devise for yourself – should be accompanied by two questions:

- Can I improve on what I've got so far?
- If so, how?

Comparing drafts is made easier if the children keep poetry folders. Such folders might contain ideas pages, first drafts, corrected drafts, final versions, sheets of teachers' notes (for example, on the drafting and editing of poems) and favourite poems by other people, both published and unpublished.

A demonstration

A good way of showing children how drafting and editing work in practice is to demonstrate the process for them. Take them through the creation of a poem, preferably one you have written yourself. If you have written the poem yourself, not only do you show how these things work, you also give some indication that poetry is more than just a school exercise: adults write, and want to write as well. You can demonstrate this by making photocopies or large charts of all the stages through which a poem has gone, showing the cuts and changes made along the way.

The idea

The first stage, the idea, may look like this:

> a teacher – tired at the end
> of the day
> the children all gone – the
> school empty
> echoing corridors
> marking still to do
> where do teachers go at
> the end of the day?

The starting point here was the question: where do teachers go at the end of the day? It is a question which springs from the mythology of teaching – that teachers are somehow different beings who never have to be excused and don't live in circumstances remotely like those known to children. This, in fact, could be the starting point for a story, so the poem might turn into a narrative of some kind. Will this mean a longish poem? We could decide not to decide about that yet. However, one decision that is needed at this stage concerns the tone we intend. It could be mysterious but is more likely to be light, faintly quizzical or odd. And what about the language? Well, since it is a poem (probably a poem) about teachers seen from a child's point of view, the language should be simple and straightforward. There should be some mystery in the poem but a mystery that is conveyed through some means other than complex language. None of these considerations is binding, and none need occupy us for long. It is quite likely that some of the questions tackled at this stage will not be consciously considered at all.

So, we are ready to make a first attempt. Or rather, in this demonstration we are ready. In an ideal world we would let the idea hang around for a while.

The first draft

> Where do teachers go when day is done?
> The corridors empty, the children all at home
> One of them is sitting still, at his desk
> A pile of marking before him like a wall.
> Any child watching now might see a glimpse
> Of the other life a teacher leads;
> Might witness the transformation
> Of teacher into ...
> Something else.

Here some of the loose ideas from the ideas stage have been threaded together to make some sort of narrative sense. This version has started to do what most writing should try to do: sharpen the focus. By this I mean that, instead of merely pondering the question 'Where do teachers go at the end of the day?', it closes in on one teacher. This is something that can always be pointed out to children. Consider ways of making your writing more specific, more particular. If they imagine themselves as a camera, you can ask them to close in on one part of the picture they have created, or even one part of the idea that is playing around in their heads. In the case of this poem, it seems that it is possible to close in even more, to make the teacher we see sitting at his desk even more particular. One way of doing this is to give him a name. We can call him Mr Parker because Parker is a fairly teacherly, reasonably ordinary sort of name.

Tinkering with the first draft

How else can we improve on this draft? (I take it for granted that we are not satisfied with it as it stands.) The next stage is to do the tinkering. Because this is a demonstration, the tinkering is made obvious. In any real attempt at a poem it is unlikely to be as clear as this. Tinkering may be done as the first draft is written: words challenged as they are set down, line endings changed before the next line is composed, and so on.

At the tinkering stage we are looking for things that might be cut, at the language, the word order, rhythm and rhyme. And, of course, anything else that strikes us as a way of improving the poem.

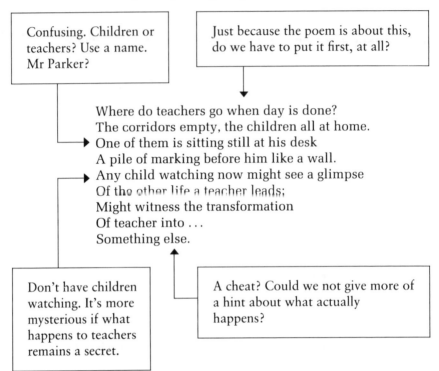

Confusing. Children or teachers? Use a name. Mr Parker?

Just because the poem is about this, do we have to put it first, at all?

Where do teachers go when day is done?
The corridors empty, the children all at home.
One of them is sitting still at his desk
A pile of marking before him like a wall.
Any child watching now might see a glimpse
Of the other life a teacher leads;
Might witness the transformation
Of teacher into . . .
Something else.

Don't have children watching. It's more mysterious if what happens to teachers remains a secret.

A cheat? Could we not give more of a hint about what actually happens?

Language: 'when day is done' – cliché, not appropriate here
'sitting still' – ambiguous
'transformation' – not a good word, spoils what rhythm there is
(The last two lines also break up the rhythm, but to greater purpose.)

The second draft

The corridor is empty, the children all at home.
Mr Parker, still sitting at his desk,
Faces a wall of books to mark.
As evening falls, Mr Parker begins to change.
He sheds his battered jacket
Stuffed with pens,
And dons instead his superhero suit.
He flies unnoticed through the evening sky.

Even in making a clear second draft from the rough notes scribbled over the first draft, you continue to question what you have written and make slight changes. Now might be a good time to compare this draft with the original notes on ideas for the poem, and with the second draft. What appears to have faded from this version is the rhythm of the first. This is partly because 'stuffed with pens' is too short to stand as a line by itself and, to a certain extent, it throws some of the other lines out. What is needed is an even, calm rhythm to the lines which will match the mood of the end of the day. Perhaps this can be achieved through changing the order of some of the words. The main problem, however, remains the poem's content. We now know what happens to Mr Parker but it doesn't come over with sufficient force. We need a device which will help us to surprise the reader slightly at Mr Parker's transformation. 'Flies' is a word that could be improved.

The final draft

These stages of tinkering and comparing drafts go on as often as is necessary. As this is a demonstration, we can cut many of them out and take a look at the poem in its final state.

Mr Parker

The children have all gone.
Dusk descends in the classroom
And Mr Parker puts down his pen
On the last marked maths book
In the pile and stretches in his chair.
Picking up his shabby case
And his whistle on a string
He shambles down the corridor
To that mysterious little room
Marked Staff Cloakroom – Men.
Seconds later Mr Parker issues forth
In sequinned leotard and tights
And climbing on the kitchen roof
Swoops home across the darkening sky.

It doesn't matter how good this poem is. If poets hesitated because falling short of perfection worried them, very little poetry would be written. What is important here is that:

a)   you help to eliminate coyness because you discuss your own work quite freely, without over-apologizing for it or giving the impression that it is precious. Coyness about what one writes can stifle the imagination. It is much more healthy, and less inhibiting, to say, 'This is the finished version. What do you think?' It gives the children a rare chance to comment on their teacher's work.

b)   you can show the kind of thinking that accompanies the making of a poem.

It is possible to go through the photocopied sheets of your poem with a class in a single session. The danger in this is that you can overlook the time that each stage may have taken to create. Few poems can be put together as quickly as one can describe the processes which may have gone into their creation. The children need to be aware of that. They also need to know how helpful it can be to test the lines as they are written; test them by saying them quietly to yourself. Much can be gained by trying the sound of words on your ear, feeling for their natural rhythm, tasting them for effect, so to speak.

If children become familiar with a method of working like this they will find it much easier to challenge what they write. They will begin to make more thoughtful choices. Drafting and editing are not natural processes for children to grasp but demonstrations like the one set out above can help them to get used to the idea of tinkering and improving. Allowing a good measure of time for poetry also helps.

Poems needn't be finished in the session in which they are started.

The list of suggestions made here is not exclusive. Neither is it one which should be adhered to at all costs. It is, however, supposed to be useful so it should be taken, adapted, cut, chopped or changed around until it works best. I would want to avoid children writing by formulae. I would want to avoid, for example, the situation in which a child is admonished for 'forgetting the second drafting stage'. Following the strict rules of drafting and editing will not create a poem. In fact there are no rules, as such, for writing creatively, and much of poetry teaching is concerned with breaking free from shackles like these. So, these are *suggestions*, and each suggestion is hedged about by provisos and warnings not to take things too seriously.

'Hear this my poem!'

(Rutooro, Africa)

10 Presenting and sharing poetry with children

Most young children enjoy sharing poetry with their friends, their class and with adults. This chapter looks at some of the ways in which schools can provide opportunities to bring children, adults and poetry together.

Through assemblies

In many schools the morning assembly provides opportunities for children to share their most recent project work with the rest of the school. In my present school Thursdays are set aside for class assemblies and the children look forward to them. It is a time when, for about half an hour, there is a captive audience of children, teachers and parents and, occasionally, governors – an ideal opportunity to present some poetry.

Because it is an integral part of any work that is going on in my classroom, the children quite naturally include poetry in their topic work. This means that any assembly I have organised has also included poetry as a natural component. I recently asked a group of children which kind of assembly they liked best. They all preferred those that involved other children. One they particularly recalled was an assembly which consisted entirely of poetry but which had come about as the result of a mistake. I had been allocated a time for my class assembly and the children were busy shaping dramatised scenes from their grandparents' lives into a concert presentation which would last about twenty minutes. We were due to perform in three weeks' time so there was no hurry to complete the work. It was after a particularly busy 'historical' session that a colleague casually mentioned that my class was due to do an assembly on the following Thursday. I rushed off to check the rota only to discover that I had obligingly swapped my day with another member of staff and had then promptly forgotten all about the arrangement! The following morning I confessed to the children. Their reactions were pre-dictable. Some moaned, some resigned themselves utterly to failure and a missed opportunity and others said wonderfully consoling things like 'We'll think of something.' So we sat in the classroom thinking and making suggestions. It was Matthew who came up with an idea that appealed to everyone. 'Why don't we just read 'em some poems'? And that is what we did.

Matthew chose two that he would read from Roger McGough's *Sky in the Pie*. This was the most recent anthology I had introduced to the children. It was very popular and other members of the class joined in, protesting that Matthew had got the best poems for himself. I suggested others from the same book and all the children were keen to be included. I spent some of that morning and the lunch-hour organising who would read what and how it should be done. The children had some very good ideas and, after about two hours work, each child had something to read, to say or to act. The assembly was now beginning to take shape but I felt that it lacked some vital component. I wanted to demonstrate to the children that poetry is created out of everyday situations, that the material they need to use for subject matter is always around them. Quite simply they need to become aware. I was really looking for a link between the poetry and the assembly. Then I read 'My Week':

My Week
This week my week started on Thursday then went
straight into TUESDAY. SUNDAY followed
looking a trifle puzzled and no wonder because
WEDNESDAY came next. MONDAY tottered in
leading SATURDAY by the morning. FRIDAY
surrendered and the week was up.

Roger McGough

How appropriately it captured the confusion and muddle I had experienced prior to the assembly and it occurred to me that most of the busy children, parents and teachers in our audience would immediately identify with the poet. I decided to use it as our opening poem, to be recited as our reason for being confused about when we were to do our assembly.

The school hall was full as my class, who normally would have been stationed at the front of the hall for such an occasion, filed in with me to take their places in the audience and and wait for the Head to introduce the proceedings. He had previously been primed of our situation and gave us a brief introduction, emphasising how eagerly the whole school was awaiting our performance. As soon as he made it clear that *our* assembly was expected, my class turned and pleaded with me to reassure them that this was not the case. I gently corrected the false impression given by the Head and endeavoured to assure him that our assembly was due in three weeks' time and would be ready then. However, by this time, the children were getting involved and one of my class called out that it was the turn of an infant class to show us *their* work. The infants were indignant, having splendidly performed for us the previous week.

To end the mounting tension I impatiently despatched a waiting child to the staffroom to bring the assembly rota to the hall. The entire audience, adults and children, waited silently while hurrying footsteps receded along the corridor towards the staff room. We all heard the door open, then close as the running footsteps retraced their passage to the hall. At last a panting child reappeared in the hall doorway waving the disputed rota. Everyone waited with bated breath as it was confirmed that it was *our* assembly after all. Then the Head turned to the class and encouraged them to do their best 'especially as we have all waited so patiently!' This was the cue for the children to get to their feet and shuffle reluctantly to the acting space at the front of the hall. I joined them and, after quietening their mock protests, I turned to apologise to the audience, telling them that the confusion was all my fault and was due mainly to the fact that I had got the days muddled. I then recited 'My Week' and sat down away from my class. This was immediately followed by a child reciting another 'My Week' poem. Then a group of children appeared and sat around a school table. On the pretext of writing their news they recited the third 'My Week' poem:

My Week

MONDAY – wrote novel, two TV plays and a book of
light verse. TUESDAY – got up early, had light breakfast
(two 50 watt bulbs), swam channel. Back in time to
watch Coronation Street. WEDNESDAY – organised
and took part in four armed robberies, in Birmingham area.
Came home with £250,000. THURSDAY laid low
played with the kids. Wrote second novel. FRIDAY –
blackmailed local Alderman at lunchtime, went to PTA
meeting at night. SATURDAY –sprang two mates from
Strangeways. Watched Match of the Day.
SUNDAY – two mates came over for dinner. Roast lamb,
carrots and turnips, jacket potatoes. Police raid during
rice pudding – went quietly.

Roger McGough

The news writers were removed by police officers. After this I 'forced' two nervous children to recite a poem they had supposedly thought of that minute. They apologetically blurted out 'The Poet's Garden'. This was followed by two girls running to the front row of the audience and asking them to guess how old they were, but it was really a recital of the poem 'Easy Money'.

Easy Money
Guess how old I am?
Bet you can't.
I bet you.
Go on guess.
Have a guess.

Wrong!
Have another.

Wrong!
Have another.

Wrong again!
Do you give in?

Seven years four months two weeks
Five days three hours fifteen
minutes forty-eight seconds!
That's 20p you owe me.

Roger McGough

Even by this time the audience still wasn't sure if we were doing a 'proper' assembly with 'proper' poems or whether we were just making things up to fill the time. Children then came on to talk about their hobbies. 'Dancin' ' was recited in this way with mime accompanying. 'Cinema Poem' by Roger McGough was recited by a group of children who kept their faces towards a projector screen and their backs to the audience – until the last line!

Cinema Poem
I like it when
They get shot in the head
And there's blood on the pillow
And blood on the bed.

And it's good when
They get stabbed in the eye
And they scream and they take
A long time to die.

And it all spurts out
All over the floor
And the audience shivers
And shouts for more.

But I don't like it when they kiss.

The next poem 'Life on Mars' begins:

> Is there life on Mars? Yes, there is. I know because
> My Auntie Pat lived there for years

We decided to set it in a hairdressing salon. Two boys, dressed as women, tottered onto the stage in high heels, and one proceeded to fix large pink rollers into the hair of the client – one was the garrulous hairdresser and the other the silent victim.

By this time it was very obvious that we had rehearsed and that we weren't giving an impromptu performance (not quite!). It was at this point that we began to introduce more serious poems. 'Tell Me Why' is a war poem and was recited by a child sitting in bed holding a teddy bear, while his father was waiting to go to war in the morning. 'Friendship Poems' were also presented seriously. Towards the end of the assembly we dramatised a reading of 'The Snowman', mimed to a reading of 'Haiku', acted out 'The Leader' and 'Sky in the Pie', and finished with all the class singing 'The Headmaster's Hymn' by Alan Ahlberg from the book *Please Mrs Butler*. For this the class group was 'conducted' by a child dressed in a teacher's gown and a mortar board. It was a very amusing ending; everyone clapped and asked for more.

When we eventually finished our singing, I thanked the school for being so patient and apologised for *not* doing an assembly. I then spent some time showing the book *Sky in the Pie* and told everyone that we had intended to do some work based on the wonderful poems in Roger McGough's book. I read out titles from the book and showed pictures and told the children that, as they were no doubt sorry to miss all these poems, they could borrow the book from me at any time. I also took the opportunity to advertise other poetry books that were for sale in my bookshop. As the children filed out of the hall at the end of assembly there were, on display, copies of *Sky in the Pie* and other poetry books which were available from the school shop.

All that day children from other classes talked to us: 'It was really an assembly, wasn't it?', 'They were real poems you learned, weren't they?' Of course, my class loved denying our frenzied preparation. Their stock answer was 'No, we forgot to do an assembly,' or 'Poems? We didn't read any poems!' My copy of *Sky in the Pie* was on permanent loan for a month after the non-assembly and I sold nine copies of the hardback book (it wasn't then available in paperback) in the shop in the following weeks. Parents came looking for 'the book with hairdressers talking about Mars' and, for about a week after the assembly, in the playground some children would entertain others with snatches of McGough poetry. Two members of staff bought the book and one granny came to buy a copy for herself: 'I don't see why the youngsters should have all the fun', she said.

In presenting poetry in the school assembly I was able to use many devices to enhance the poems and to heighten their impact on a captive audience with an age-range of five to about seventy. Because McGough speaks very directly to the reader it is easy to recite his poems. There is in *Sky in the Pie* a conversational, intimate tone which the audience can enjoy. The halting, diffident start to our assembly was designed to alienate those watching so that our apologies, explanations and revelations would have a more dramatic effect. By the time we attempted more serious poems the audience was beginning to trust us.

During the twenty minute assembly we used various devices. These were miming to narration, dramatised readings and choral speaking. Dance was used and, at the end of the session, I spent a few minutes talking about the poetry and the books. This was an important part of the assembly because I particularly wanted to share the *books* with the audience, hoping that, if the poems had spoken directly to the children, there would be evidence they were reading the books long after I had finished talking.

Reading to children

An assembly, concert or similar event is one way of presenting poetry to a large audience. Presenting poetry to a class also needs careful preparation but benefits from the intimacy of established relationships. Another significant advantage is that the presentation usually takes place in a setting which you can take time to create. In my own classroom I spend a considerable amount of time and effort creating conditions in which children can learn. However small the room, so far I have managed to create a corner in which all the children can relax, sitting on an area of carpet or on a cushion they may have made themselves. It is important that the children feel that they own their reading corner, so I invite them to decorate the walls with their paintings, make cushions, provide material and plants and decide how we should display books and arrange the seating. This, for me, is an area where most of the class books are kept and where all newly-acquired books, from home or school, are on view for everyone to see. It is the place I choose to present all new books to a class, and it becomes the focus of the room where important things are shown, discussed, related and shared. At any given time during the day the reading area could be used for discussing the attributes of an isosceles triangle or the characteristics of a particular author. Throughout the day it is used for group and individual activities, but is especially important when I want to share something significant with the class group.

In the classroom where poetry is given status, there will always be spontaneous reading of a newly-discovered poem and I have occasionally stopped an activity so that a child could read out a particularly amusing or appropriate few lines for the class to enjoy. However, usually, the reading of poetry is less spontaneous and is prepared by me or by the children in advance. There are obvious reasons for this that involve the careful selection and preparation of the readings themselves. I often choose a particular theme or author and usually link the poetry with relevant topic work, or use it to stimulate children's thinking before embarking upon new work.

An important element in the preparation of readings is the consideration of *when* to read to a class. The best time varies considerably and depends upon many factors. For example, I once had a reading area that overlooked the school football field. I therefore always planned to read in the mornings before a practice or a match, or in the afternoon when it was raining (but this usually meant last minute planning at lunchtime). Another reading area I created had thirty children lining up for swimming lessons outside against the windows. They appeared every thirty minutes during a two-hour session on days when the summer temperature crept above 60°F. That summer I read quite a few short poems to small groups so that everyone managed to get a fair share in the discussion.

Most teachers reading this will also have similar problems to contend with and will, perhaps, identify with the enthusiastic presenter of poetry who is trying to find a few quiet moments in the busy school day. My favourite time for reading to a class is early morning. I find that this is the best time because the children seem to be at their most calm and receptive at this time of the day. Also the school is generally quieter and there are fewer interruptions. (No one is making enquiries about lost socks because at 9.15 they have yet to be lost!) And if the readings require explanation and discussion you have the whole day ahead of you to answer questions and follow up lines of enquiry.

Obviously there are other good times for reading to children and each school and each particular class will have its own set of circumstances which will dictate these best times. I know that a popular time for reading to children is at the end of the school day. I also use this session, but rarely for introducing new poetry or fiction that requires a good deal of discussion and explanation. I do use it as a time for old favourites and for the children to talk about poetry they particularly enjoy. There are times in the school day when I have learned to avoid introducing poetry. I find the most difficult time to engage the children's interest is after wet breaks, especially after wet lunchtimes, and in my experience children who have just had a swimming lesson are at their least receptive to the delights of poetry!

Finding the best time to read to your class also means that you must be aware of your best time as a reader. Again I find that the children's mood and my enthusiasm happily coincide early in the day. Once you begin to know a class well you gain in confidence with reading and can begin to tackle different accents. Listening to radio drama has helped me to improve and, if you are unsure, the children will help. There are usually a few gifted mimics in any class or you may be lucky enough to have children who naturally speak with an accent. I have always found such children to be delightfully helpful, patient and amused at my inept pronunciation. You might even be able to persuade one or two to join you in a particular reading.

Reading aloud to a group of children is not an easy option. I now find it one of the most enjoyable aspects of teaching and one of the most satisfying.

However, unless it comes naturally to you (and it does to some) then it is a skill that has to be learned. As a student teacher I found reading to a class difficult. My lack of confidence inhibited any experimenting with different tones, inflections and accents. I thought that the children would be unconvinced by my attempts and the result was that I read rather monotonously and the children became bored and listless. I remember realising just how poor I was when I watched an experienced teacher read 'Matilda' by Hilaire Belloc. I do remember thinking that I could never be so at ease, so accomplished, but I noted those things I could improve on. Firstly, I noticed how much an experienced reader looks at the audience, specially when turning over a page. There is never a pause due to the mechanics of the process. However, I did note that meaningful pauses could be surprisingly long. I realised that there was no need to rush and that, used skilfully, silence was as important as the spoken word.

Where the reader sits in relation to the audience is also important. For this reason, I have always tried to make the reading area in my classroom as large as is practically possible. Ideally, it should be large enough to accommodate all the children comfortably at one time. I also prefer everyone to be able to see my face when I am reading. Eye-contact is important and so is facial expression. You do need to be able to see all of the children, and they need to see you. Then, if you are really communicating, you will know simply by exchanging glances with your audience.

Tapes and records

I originally acquired tapes and records of poetry because I was eager to hear how professional readers used their skills. There were relatively few when I first began to build up a library but now there is a wide range available and these are often obtainable from your local library. In my early years as a teacher I used these recordings simply for my own pleasure, then a few years ago I began to use them in the classroom with groups of children. I am very selective and normally only use a small section of a tape or record with a group of children. It can be difficult for some children to give their undivided attention to a disembodied voice so I spend quite a long time preparing the group for this. I also ensure that there will be the minimum of interruption and have therefore sometimes worked away from the classroom with a small group while the rest of the class has been busy with another teacher. These are rare opportunities now and, more recently, I have used time during the lunch-hour for such an activity.

I prepare the children by writing down the title and author of the poem and telling them a little about the poet, or anything else that might be significant or interesting to them. I tell them that I shall ask them a few questions after their first hearing. In this way I endeavour to focus their attention. I then suggest that they may like to close their eyes while listening. This makes it easier for children to ignore extraneous distractions and they more quickly 'tune in' to their mental images. I have always asked children to pretend that there is a film going on inside their heads when they are listening to poetry, fiction or music. Although occasionally some children have 'blank screens' or do not wish to tell you about their images, eventually they do become responsive and let you glimpse into their imaginations. But this doesn't always happen unless there is sensitive questioning.

In a group where children are genuinely creating meaning and significance through poetic language, there must be an atmosphere which is non-threatening and non-competitive, in which every child is attended to as a serious contributor to group discussion and poetry writing. It is essential to treat each child as a person capable of making important statements about poetry and as capable of producing significant poetry. Each child must trust that what she says or writes is going to be listened to and appreciated by other members of the class or group. But there must also be respect for the fact that writing and responding to poetry are essentially *private* acts and that some children will, at times, not wish to venture an opinion or read their own poetry to the class. The best responses (and the best poems) always come when trust and respect are fostered positively in a group of children. Real communication only develops where good relationships and mutual respect exist. Obviously, it takes a long time to achieve this in a busy and creative classroom, and a great deal of patient understanding and emotional energy are required. The kind of small group work I have described does help to foster positive attitudes. It teaches children how to listen to poetry and how to listen to others.

Tapes made by children

There are many ways of presenting poetry to children and one of the most successful that I have tried is to produce tapes with them. I started this when I was teaching in a large junior school and wanted to advertise my newly-opened bookshop. I put a selection of books together in an attractive box and made a tape of extracts and reviews of these books. This 'book box' was then on loan to classes during the period immediately prior to the bookshop sessions. It was the children in my class at the time who suggested that they should make the tapes and eventually they began to produce their own recommendations, reviews and readings. To make recording easier we decided upon a poetry box and a fiction box. This has now expanded and a reference box is in progress and will eventually be on loan to all library users.

The poetry tapes have proved to be the most popular. Most of the children enjoy choosing a poem that they will record and I produce a list of these so that the poems can be appropriately grouped under subject matter or author or even under form: haiku, limerick, sonnet, ballad. The children then decide how they will go about the recording – sometimes they work individually, more often in pairs and occasionally in groups of up to six. I spend quite a lot of time discussing each chosen poem. In fact, the choosing often takes a while but it is a very important part of the whole process. The children spend a long time poring over the anthologies in the classroom and their earnest discussion about the merits of one poem over another are often very revealing and would surprise a more seasoned critic! After the final choice is made the children discuss how to present their particular poem. Some children do actually choose to record their own poetry writing and occasionally a classroom poet will allow her work to be performed by others in the class. This ensures a wide variety of poetry recorded on tape and provides teachers and children with a source of poems which is immediately accessible and personal. I have a collection of such tapes and use them often.

Using music ...

One of the most effective ways of enhancing poetry for use with young children is to produce music that will complement it and emphasise its meaning. I have been especially keen to experiment with this after working with John Agard at a poetry workshop. Children were enchanted by his music-making and his rhythmic refrains and they enthusiastically participated. I have tried to recreate this atmosphere in the classroom and some children have responded by producing their own music to accompany poetry on tape. This is particularly effective when used with limericks and short humorous verse but the children have also produced some rather haunting, more serious music to accompany children's poetry about the sea. It is not necessary to have a wide variety of musical instruments. With simple percussion children can be very inventive and it is exciting and interesting to improvise.

and dance ...

I have also used these poetic and musical experiences to stimulate children into creating movement. Some animal poetry can be successfully performed in this way. I once worked with second year juniors on the theme of 'seasons' and found that they created wonderful sounds and movement to accompany their own voices, reading published poetry and their own. With a group of thirteen-year-olds I worked on the theme of 'the elements' and, using some sound effects from the BBC's radiophonic workshop, they created poetry, music and movement which held and audience spellbound for three quarters of an hour.

and mime ...

Mime is closely allied to dance in the context of presenting poetry, in that it should silently add to the spoken word, not draw attention away from the poetry. As in all these activities, the poetry is central and each art form should complement it, not overshadow it in any way. When I use mime with poetry I endeavour to keep both elements simple. This is because timing is important and if badly done the poetry can be lost. A simple yet effective mime was used in the Roger McGough assembly. Two children faced the audience and one recited 'Haiku' while the other, dressed in scarf and with a carrot nose, slowly melted away

Haiku
Snowman in a field
Listening to the raindrops
Wishing him farewell

Roger McGough

The timing had to be right for the poetry to work, the last word spoken as the drops of rain melt the last little heap of snow. The 'snowman' confessed to me that as she finally melted she heard some infants whisper, 'Ah, he's gone' so she knew her mime had been convincing.

and drama . . .

Another way of presenting poetry to children is by using drama. This is not the dramatised reading that I mentioned earlier as part of the assembly, but a form of expression that exists independently of the poem even though it is derived from it. I am thinking of such narrative poems as 'The Gresford Disaster' which tells a powerful story. This is true of all narrative poems. They may not celebrate real events in history but they tell stories that can be told in other equally valid ways. I have rewritten and then dramatised 'The Pied Piper of Hamelin' and have created music and dance for a retelling of 'The Lady of Shalott'. To be successful in dramatic form, a poem should have a strong story line. You are at liberty to use the story and to tell it through the medium of drama but it is important to acknowledge your source and to bring it to the attention of all those who may watch your new version of an old tale.

and art . . .

In the chapter which deals with using 'The Rime of the Ancient Mariner' as the basis for a term's work, I mention that artwork featured prominently. In that particular project the art and craft took a long time and was the result of extensive planning and organisation. Usually, the work is spontaneous and takes only an allotted session. I first became aware of the potential of using haiku poems in the classroom when I was browsing through a poetry book containing small but equisitely detailed paintings which accompanied the poetry. The scale of the poems and that of the artwork seemed to balance each other perfectly. I now have a collection of paintings on postcards and use these when I am talking about how haiku works. Within a poetry session I only use a few poems if I am also introducing the option of artwork. Perhaps three haiku would be a maximum in the first session – usually varying in subject matter to give everyone a choice.

Animals are popular subjects for artwork and there are numerous poems that invite illustration. I have found that children often begin by drawing cartoons or illustrating humorous poems – the drawings from *First Book of Poems*, edited by John Foster, are always popular and I am happy to allow children to copy these at first. This is because some children are diffident about their ability to draw freely and they can gain confidence from seeing a well-executed copy of someone else's work. With patient persuasion and much encouragement from the teacher, it is possible to convince the less confident child to attempt some original artwork, particularly if you choose poems with care, knowing they will appeal to those who need such encouragement.

By display

Displaying poetry and associated art and craftwork is a very important aspect of teaching. Perhaps it could be classed as part of the hidden curriculum of the primary school environment. In my teaching I point out to children that poetry is to be found in everyday situations and I draw their attention to their own rich and natural figurative language. Another way of drawing children's attention to poetry is to display it where they habitually congregate, for example, a notice board near a dinner queue. In my own school this particular display does tend to get torn and dog-eared but over a hundred children look at the work once a day at least so it is a good place to put poetry. It is important, however, to place the written work where it can be read by small children. So often, when visiting schools, I notice that attractive drawings and interesting poetry are well out of the reach of young children's hands. I can understand the reluctance of teachers to leave work in a vulnerable position but, if it is to be appreciated by the rest of the school, then it must be in a place where it can be viewed properly. You can teach children to respect the work of others and one of the best ways of doing this is to station your poets and artists near their displayed material. They can then talk about their work and prevent sticky hands from spoiling the finished product!

Another very successful place for displaying poetry is also a very unlikely one – the cloakrooms and toilets of a school. I once taught in a small room adjoining a cavernous church hall. My first year juniors had to make a daring journey along a dark corridor before they reached the green-tiled toilets at the end. Using Michael Rosen's poem 'The Longest Journey in the World' as a stimulus, I asked the children to write about their longest journey. Most of them quite naturally wrote about the corridor to the toilets, as I had expected, and I displayed their poetry and pictures all along that corridor and in the toilets. This had the desired effect of dispelling their fears although it increased the number of journeys. However, it did make me realise what a lot of wasted display space there is in school toilets. It seems that, whatever one does to prevent it, many children spend a great deal of their time there, especially in winter lunchtimes. A few pictures and poems might actually be noticed more than in a busy classroom – and there is always the possibility that your school caretaker might find them a cheerful addition to the decor!

It is important to display poetry where visitors to the school offices will be able to read it. There are two main reasons for this. Firstly, I think visitors should see that the school gives status to poetry in the curriculum; that it is regarded as an essential element in a child's education. Secondly, it is important to make everyone aware of the quality of the poetry that local children are capable of producing. I have often spent time convincing sceptical parents that their child did not copy a published poem and pass it off as her own. Displaying a range of poetry writing from a year group or a class does make visitors more aware of the general standard of creative writing throughout the school, and it can help others realise that getting children to create poetry is more than providing an idea, the paper and pencils. I once displayed the children's draft and final poems alongside photographs of famous poets' first and final versions. The writing attracted a lot of attention and provoked such comments as: 'It makes you realise it's not as easy as it looks.' It is always good to feel that people appreciate the complexity of the writing process. Sometimes a display can do more than lengthy conversations to help people understand these difficulties. But conversations can help, especially those with poets...

Visiting poets

During the past five years I have made use of an excellent scheme which seeks to bring professional writers and children together in the classroom. The scheme operates under the auspices of the Regional Arts Associations and local associations are listed in the telephone directory. Local teachers' centres will also help to put you in touch with the scheme. Once you have made contact, the literature officer will supply you with information about who is available and will help you to match a poet to your requirements. For this reason it is a good idea to think carefully about the needs and abilities of your class or group before you invite a poet. You will then be more able to specify what you hope to achieve and an experienced literature officer will suggest poets suitable for your particular group. Funding for this scheme does vary, but most Associations will pay for all or part of the poet's fee. Schools have to provide expenses. It is therefore wise to choose a poet from your locality if you can, for this reduces travelling expenses.

Some writers prefer to work independently of teachers but others enjoy working with them relying on their knowledge of the children. I prefer to be involved with the work but if I have not been asked to participate as a teacher, I then participate as a writer. It is a useful way to learn more about the craft of writing from the pupils' viewpoint, and also to experience the vulnerability of the writer. Participation in this way has shown me how much it helps children to present some of your own writing in a group where there are helpful and constructive comments. I have always found that, in this way, relationships of mutual trust and respect develop and writing flourishes.

If you are not able to have a poet visiting your school, it may be possible for your class to visit a poet. Many journals and magazines advertise local book events and you can reserve places for workshop sessions in local halls, libraries and community centres. These are less intimate occasions than working with a poet in the classroom but they are usually great fun and can involve music and dancing as well as poetry. Often large numbers of children attend festival events and there is the chance to share poetry with other local schools.

Festivals and events

Of course it is possible to create a poetry event in your own school. This can be done on a large scale involving the entire school population, or it can simply be a small event which you organise with your own class. The large scale event is very exciting and worthwhile but it does require an immense amount of time and energy. It is a good idea to enlist the help of staff and parents and to delegate certain jobs right from the beginning of the project. Regular meetings between the organisers ensure that everyone is kept informed of progress as the event gathers momentum. I find the best time for such ventures is at the beginning of the academic year, when staff and children are more likely to be relaxed and enthusiastic after the summer break. I have usually timed poetry events to coincide with Children's Book Week in October. This gives me about six weeks from the beginning of term to plan.

There are many exciting things that can be included in a school-based poetry event. I have listed below some of the most successful that I have organised or been involved in:

Competitions

These generate enthusiasm and interest and I have tended to keep them light-hearted, providing small prizes for the participants. The Parent Teachers Association has usually granted a sum of money to defray costs. There have been:

- poetry quizzes for adults
- poetry quizzes for children – one for infants and one for juniors
- family poetry quizzes
- a limerick competition for parents and children
- guess the poet – a competition requiring entrants to match poets and their poems

- guess the teacher's favourite poem – poems and teachers' names have to be matched
- unjumble the poets' names

There are many more and teachers will no doubt think of their own.

Exhibitions

Here are some suggestions for exhibitions:
- a display of illustrations of favourite poems
- a display of designs for a favourite anthology
- books, posters, photographs all based upon a particular poetry theme, for example the sea, animals, night or home

You may find that your local bookseller will allow you to have books on a sale or return basis. They may be prepared to come along at the time of the event, advise parents and children in their choice of poetry books and help you to sell them. Local librarians will also often come to help and their knowledge can be very useful. They are usually interested in exhibitions of work and are often very grateful for the loan of your particular display of work in the children's public library. Good relationships between schools and local libraries can be mutually helpful and promote poetry in and out of the school context.

School newspapers and magazines

Another way to take poetry out of the immediate context of the school is by producing it in newspapers or school magazines which are available to a wide audience. I have reservations about such publications having known children who, however hard they try, have never had their poems printed. Children (and parents!) do regard the inclusion of their work as a yardstick of their success and, being concerned to foster writing talent at all levels, I have been sorry when children whose work is not included in magazines have lost confidence and sometimes refused to write. On the other hand, I greatly enjoy reading booklets and magazines from other schools and use them extensively in my own poetry teaching, either as material for the children to read or as a source book of ideas that might work with my own class.

Personal books and individual folders

One way of overcoming the problem of competition and rivalry is to ask the children to produce their own magazine or folder, including their favourite drawings, poetry and illustrations. I have usually asked everyone to keep a folder of their favourite poetry over the year and spend time during the first week of term producing very individual folders with the children. Some choose to tie-dye material for their covers, others use iron-on crayon designs, screenprinting techniques or lino-cut to print on paper or cotton covers. A few children can never decide and leave their designs until inspiration comes later in the year. These are often the most successful, the designs usually being inspired by poems the children become familiar with as the term progresses. Eventually, all the children have a finished cover but they begin their collection of well-loved poems in the first week of the new school year.

Young children include poetry they enjoyed when they were very young, others copy out short passages from poems they don't fully understand yet – as long as I am satisfied that the child really enjoys the poetry then that is all that matters. Most children become very involved in this work during the year and it is interesting to see how their tastes develop and how important their poetry folders become. The children also keep a folder or a book of their own poetry writing and occasionally one of their own poems is copied out to go into the folder of favourites. I am always pleased when this happens, as when they copy out a friend's poem for their own collection.

I have also kept a collection of class favourites and have produced an anthology to be displayed in the reading area. The system was that any poem that did not receive at least half the class votes could not be included. The children were encouraged to copy out and present each individual poem as well as they could. Usually each child was invited to choose the colour of the mounting paper and to talk about her proposed layout for the presentation. Occasionally I typed out poems for the children, particularly if they were keen to have a typed poem as part of the design of the entire page. All the anthologies, individual or collective, became books to be admired and treasured. I have a large collection of these and find they are very useful source books: the children really appreciate browsing through them, enjoying the poetry and the artwork that complements it.

Using television and radio

There is an increasing number of excellent broadcasts which stimulate children's enthusiasm for poetry. I have used most of those available at the time of writing and am impressed by the generally high standard. My particular preference is for radio. Non-visual stimuli can often evoke very powerful images and good radio broadcasts can help to develop a child's capacity for imagining. If possible, it is always best to record the programmes. You can then decide upon their suitability and can prepare how best to use them in the classroom – you can edit, repeat poems and use the tape again. The programmes become so much more useful and versatile once recorded and I have usually kept the best of these for the permitted three years. Radio tapes are easier to use with small groups than pre-recorded television. A school video is usually based in a room away from the classroom and it is more difficult to organise group viewing if your children have to leave the classroom in order to watch the programme. If you only want to work with a group, using a video tape in the classroom inevitably means that the other children are distracted.

There are television programmes not specifically designed to stimulate poetry that are a very good source of material. I have used a science programme and a history series to promote poetry writing. Other broadcasts which have been beautifully filmed, particularly those on animals, have successfully inspired the children into writing although they weren't originally made for children. When the annual radio and television programme details appear, I can never decide which broadcasts to use and usually err on the side of caution by ordering more pamphlets than I really need. These are relatively inexpensive and provide printed poems and some good suggestions for writing activities. I use the pamphlets often, even if I don't use the programmes.

National poetry competitions

While radio and television programmes stimulate children to create poetry and occasionally provide competitions for their audiences, there are an increasing number of national competitions for children to enter. 'Junior Education' and 'The Times Educational Supplement' have details of current competitions. Three annual competitions for children are:

The W. H. Smith Children's Literary Competition
The Cadbury's Poetry Competition
The Observer Poetry Competition

The standard for national competitions is high and it is important to talk to would-be entrants about this so that they aren't too disappointed when they don't win prizes. In all of these competitions there are certificates and prizes both for individuals and for schools. Every year the organisers publish a book containing the winning entries.

'What we call the beginning is often the end
And to make an end is to make a beginning.
The end is where we start from.'

(T. S. Eliot)

11 An end and a beginning

A person's first encounter with poetry often means more than can be calculated at the time. While we were working on *In tune with yourself*, we began to think about the ways in which we first came across poetry. They seemed ordinary enough: nothing spectacular, no great sophistication, no flashes of insight and no childish visions of a path that must be taken. And yet they were beginnings, and they contained the roots of what we now feel and think about poetry – and, by extension, about a lot of other things as well – as we sit down to write about it today. It seemed to us apt to conclude the book with these recollections. Our hope now is that the end of *In tune with yourself* will mark the beginning of a personal journey for our readers.

'As a young child I had always enjoyed the poetry that was available to me and I clearly remember a book of alliterative verse in which a duck-billed platypus featured prominently. I loved the sound of words and would make up rhymes to accompany my footsteps or the sound of a tennis ball bouncing against the garden shed. I have early memories of a small garden that my father created for me and I remember being aware of the extraordinary, delightful names of the flowers I grew there – antirrhinums, forget-me-nots, marigolds and, best of all, peonies. Such lovely sounds.

Later, when I was at junior school, I can recall standing behind my small chair at the end of the day, eyes tightly shut and hands clasped. I was reciting these words:

Now the day is over,
Night is drawing nigh.
Shadows of the evening
Steal across the sky.

I must have said this verse every day for about two years but it never lost its appeal, especially those last two lines. There was something exciting about shadows that stole the day time from us. However, it wasn't until I was a top junior that I became aware of the strange, mystical power of poetry. For me this came about in a rather dramatic way.

In my primary school every top junior girl had to play the recorder in assembly. We accompanied the headmaster who played the violin. I was not looking forward to this because I much preferred to sing and, once elevated to the recorder-playing ranks, I was excluded from all singing activities. Even worse, all the school recorders were dipped in a milky solution of disinfectant before they were issued and I hated the taste of it, especially at morning assembly after a hurried breakfast. One morning the recorders were doused in a particularly strong solution of Dettol and, as I placed the instrument to my lips, I uttered a cry of disgust and spat the offending solution onto the back of a fellow musician who protested loudly. My timing had been perfect. The headmaster, with the sense of occasion of a concert violinist, had been about to position his bow and lead us into the first hymn. The commotion in the second row interrupted his heightened concentration and he opened his eyes and caught me laughing. I was ordered to leave the room. I had to pass the ensuing twenty minutes in the adjoining classroom in silent seclusion. I heard the assembly make a halting start and wandered about trying not to think of the encounter that would inevitably take place.

As I passed the teacher's desk (this was the headmaster's classroom) I noticed a music book open at the hymn I should have been playing. I had never seen the words before, only the music in the recorder books. Through the door came the strains of the remaining players gallantly piping the first few bars of "Jerusalem". I stood behind the headmaster's desk and sang my heart out to an audience of empty desks and chairs. As long as the violin kept playing I was safe! It was during those glorious few moments that I realised poetry and music could affect me profoundly; that they could arouse and quell strong emotions I had no words to describe. I remember being delighted to find adjectives in the wrong place. "Countenance divine" sounded like a phrase from a foreign language. I was stirred by the alliteration of "bring me my bow of burning gold" and the phrase "arrows of desire" rang in my head for days. That afternoon I was told to return the school recorder to the music teacher for good. My love of poetry began the day my music education ended.' *Jennifer Dunn*

'Although I spent no time in contemplation of the matter when I was a child, there were four things which I found immediately attractive about poetry. These were the pictures it created in my mind, the sound of certain words, its occasional air of mystery, and its strong rhythms. I found them not only in the poems which had official school approval but also in playground rhymes and the language that was in use all around me. Of course, it would not have occurred to me to classify playground rhymes and ordinary speech as Poetry with a capital P, nevertheless, I heard and thought about them just as I heard and thought about poems that were presented at school.

The first poems I can recall hearing at junior school were "Drake's Drum", by Sir Henry Newbold, and "When icicles hang by the wall", from Shakespeare's *Love's Labour Lost*. Both lodged very clear *pictures* in my head. In the first, I saw a red-bearded swashbuckler asleep in a hammock slung improbably between two pyramids of cannon balls. In the second, I had a vivid image of "greasy Joan" at work scouring the bottom of a large black cauldron. These pictures reappeared whenever the poems were read. "Nombre Dios Bay" and "round-shot" were words which both sounded attractive and spoke of a mysterious world beyond the familiar. The Shakespeare also had the attraction of being by Shakespeare. Shakespeare was something the grown-ups knew about. He belonged to their world. Hearing of him in the junior school was a little like dressing up in adult clothes. This is a shame because some Shakespeare is simple direct and accessible to junior school children.

I came across many playground rhymes and they, in most cases, also conjured up vivid pictures. For example, the following brought to mind images of Louis Wain cats wielding sinister rolling pins and knocking at the front door:

> Not last night but the night before
> Two tom cats came knocking at my door.
> I went downstairs to let them in;
> They knocked me down with a rolling pin.
> The rolling pin was made of glass.
> A bit flew off and chipped my arse.

Much of the attraction of this was in its powerful rhythm, which is more subtle than at first seems to be the case. It is also clever in the way it builds up its surreal world of gangland cats, saving its rude word – mild by today's standards, but the raison d'être of the verse when it was popular in schools of the fifties – till the last line. The very fact that a rhyme like that would have been frowned on by adults added to its appeal.

At about the same time that I was hearing poems about Drake, the hardships of winter and those threatening cats, I was also becoming fascinated by the *sound* of words. These words did not have to appear in poems. "Tub", for example, was a pleasing word which sounded just like the heavy, thick lids used on ice-cream carts in which, of course, ice-cream tubs were kept. I idled away plenty of time thinking about words like this. However, this sort of speculation, like the playground rhymes, was thought to have little to do with what schools called writing. What schools called writing was Fine Writing; good descriptive words, a certain resonance, never starting a sentence with "and" or "but" and so on. Now it seems to me a pity that I was not encouraged to make use of the language around me: the sharp and sometimes ugly East End sounds, or the wonderful rhythms and words of Norfolk. Norfolk is a gift of a language to story-tellers.

Today, I love the simple and direct poems of people like Robert Frost.

However, I can still summon up the pictures I saw in my head as a child; the very same images, touched off by the same words.' *Nick Warburton*

'When I was quite young, about six, my parents went to India with my two sisters leaving me in the care of friends of the family: six sisters, all unmarried. Although the "aunts" were kind to me, they had no real understanding of children and this was a very unhappy period of my life. I felt as if I was abnormal, knew I wasn't like other children and thought it was my fault in some way. I turned inward, as many children do faced with an incomprehensible situation. In particular, I turned to books.

I gobbled up novels for children, reading indiscriminately, living vicariously through my heroines. I also discovered poetry. Unfortunately, I can't remember which poems moved or amused me, except for Robert Louis Stevenson's *A Child's Garden of Verse*. Here was somebody else who knew what it was like to feel lonely, to feel different from other children; someone else who found pleasure in solitary pursuits, yet longed for contact with people. Of course, I couldn't have articulated it so clearly then, but I have no doubt that this was the source of Stevenson's appeal. I felt a real connection with another person, though he was removed from me in time and space, through the medium of poetry. I got to know him intimately through his poems. I also loved the poems for their quietly reassuring content and strong rhythms. It was a great joy to me when I became a mother myself to find that my small son also adored the poems and demanded their repetition night after night.

Even now, when I read the last poem in the sequence, my eyes prickle up with tears.

> So you may see, if you will look
> Through the windows of this book,
> Another child, far, far away,
> And in another garden play.
> But do not think you can at all,
> By knocking on the window, call
> That child to hear you ...
> For, long ago, the truth to say,
> He has grown up and gone away,
> And it is but a child of air
> That lingers in the garden there.
>
> Robert Louis Stevenson

When I began teaching, faced with my very first class lesson, I found myself teaching poetry. I was surprised to discover it was poetry I wanted to do. Nothing in my P.G.C.E. course had highlighted poetry. However, the children were receptive, wrote with enthusiasm, and my future career was set. I have been concentrating on children and poetry ever since.

Writing this piece forced me to consider why poetry was so central to my educational beliefs. It is simply this – poetry, as well as doing many other things, helps us understand ourselves and others better, helps us grow as people, teaches us how to live. I was sustained by poetry when I was little and I want to pass on this resource to the children I teach. I know it is a resource that will last them all their lives.' *Morag Styles*

Appendix 1 and 2 contain some of the authors' favourite anthologies for use with children. Restrictions of space and the need for balance have necessitated the exclusion of many good poetry books. We regret the omissions; the lists offer a *sample* of some of the best poetry available for children at the time of writing.

Appendix 1
Some good anthologies for the classroom

1. *The Sun Dancing*, edited by Charles Causley (Puffin, 1984)
   This book of Christian verse for children is illustrated by Charles Keeping whose work is often provocative and disturbing – a very gifted artist. And Causley's poems are not dull, dutiful and conventionally religious. He has ranged widely through English poetry and beyond for this thoughtful collection.

2. *A Very First, First, Second, Third, Fourth and Fifth Poetry Book*, edited by John Foster (O.U.P.)
   With six poetry books in this series to his credit, John Foster continues to produce anthologies of quality. He uses plenty of modern poetry, including the commissioning of new poems from distinguished poets. The books are all attractively presented and packed with interesting material.

3. *Writing Poems*, edited by Michael Harrison and Christopher Stuart-Clark (O.U.P., 1985)
   Obviously a successful partnership. You may know these authors' earlier anthologies, *Poems 1* and *Poems 2* (O.U.P.). Although the title of this book is *Writing Poems*, it contains both an anthology of well-chosen poetry and ideas for pupils' own writing. It will appeal to junior and middle pupils and is good to look at as well.

4. *Poets In Hand*, edited by Anne Harvey (Puffin, 1985)
   Anne Harvey provides a selection of poetry by four living poets: Causley, Fuller, Jennings and Scannell, and the late John Walsh. She also writes about the lives and interests of her chosen poets. A good introduction to their work.

5. *The Rattle Bag*, edited by Seamus Heaney and Ted Hughes (Faber, 1982)
   This anthology is a brilliant, haphazard amalgam of a very wide range of

fine poetry: traditional and modern; English, European, American, etc. Although the book is aimed at older readers, you will find it full of possibilities for the junior and middle classroom. Reading this book is a poetic education in itself.

6. *Rhyme Time 2*, edited by Barbara Ireson (Beaver, 1984)
   I chose this particular anthology as it is so good for younger children. But any of Barbara Ireson's books are worth considering, as she is an anthologist of great experience and flair, with a particular feeling for the infant age group.

7. *Messages*, edited by Naomi Lewis (Faber, 1985)
   Here is an anthology of depth and richness by Naomi Lewis, the writer and critic. It combines some of the best English poetry, familiar to many adults, with less well-known examples from Europe, China, Japan and elsewhere. A good book for anyone who enjoys poetry, and used selectively there is material suitable for younger children. My only criticism is that, though it is aimed at middle and lower secondary readers, the presentation and layout is only likely to attract highly literate pupils.

8. *Strictly Private*, by Roger McGough (Puffin, 1982)
   A lively and stimulating selection of poetry geared to top juniors upwards. McGough chooses some 'old favourites' but most of the poems will be new to young readers. Nothing stuffy here!

9. *A Flock of Words*, edited by David Mackay (Bodley Head, 1969)
   If I could only have one anthology to use with children, this would probably be it. Despite being nearly twenty years old, it is still an invigorating read. More for the teacher to use with the children than the young reader herself. Mackay's knowledge of poetry, past and present, from all over the world is impressive. The poems are chosen with great care, one following the other harmoniously.

10. *Poems for Seven and Under*, edited by Helen Nicoll (Puffin, 1984)
    Very well chosen poems for younger children, illustrated by the talented Michael Foreman in black and white. Pleasant to look at, this is a book with lots of appeal for lower juniors and below. It is a pity Nicoll concentrates almost exclusively on male, English poets, but otherwise a fine achievenemt.

11. *This Way Delight*, edited by Herbert Read (Faber, 1957)
    A priceless book – one of the best collections of poetry for children of all time. Some of the great names of English literature feature strongly. Blake, Shakespeare, Tennyson, Shelley and such like. Herbert Read shares his delight in poetry with young readers; no talking down or compromising here, his respect for his audience is evident.

12. *The Kingfisher Book of Children's Poetry*, edited by Michael Rosen (Kingfisher Books, 1985)
    A lovely book and very good value in hardback. Michael Rosen,

probably the best loved poet for children writing today, demonstrates his skill and flair for choosing poetry in all its guises: rhymes, riddles, jokes, ballads, limericks and nonsense verse alongside poetry of seriousness and impact. A most original selection.

13. *I Like That Stuff* and *You'll Love This Stuff!*, edited by Morag Styles (C.U.P., 1984 and 1987)
Two of the very few anthologies geared to junior and middle children which draw on poetry from a wide range of cultures. The editor concentrates on African, Asian, Caribbean and black British poetry. There is a marvellous introduction to the first book by the distinguished Caribbean poet, Edward Kamau Brathwaite. Most of the poems will be new to British readers.

14. *Junior Voices 1, 2, 3* and *4*, edited by Geoffrey Summerfield (Penguin, 1970)
These books still look up-to-date, inviting and exciting both in terms of the poetry and the illustrations. Summerfield's wide knowledge of poetry is evident and the books display the sure touch of a truly creative writer and educator.

15. *Out of the Blue*, edited by Fiona Waters (Fontana Lion, 1982)
An excellent selection of poetry relating to weather. Fiona Waters avoids the obvious, no easy task given the theme, and chooses many appealing, thoughtful, and sometimes unusual poems. See also her *Golden Apples*, highly recommended by Signal 1985.

16. *I Like This Poem*, edited by Kaye Webb (Puffin, 1979)
Originally produced to celebrate The International Year of the Child, this book continues to be popular with pupils and teachers alike. Kaye Webb allows children to choose their favourite poems for themselves and say *why* they liked them. Mainly well known poetry with a few surprises.

17. *Poems for Nine and Under* and *Poems for Ten and Over*, edited by Kit Wright (Puffin, 1985)
The only dull thing about these anthologies is their titles! Companion volume to the Nicoll, also illustrated by Foreman, they contain a delightful choice of poetry. Wright has worked extensively with children over the years and this understanding, combined with his enthusiasm for poetry, makes for a winning formula.

And finally a few anthologies of poetry written by children:

18. *Cadbury's Book of Children's Poetry* (annual since 1984)

19. *Children as Writers*, anthologies from the annual W. H. Smith Literary Competitions

20. *Schools Poetry Review*, which produces an anthology every year

Appendix 2
Collections by good poets writing for children

1. John Agard
   I Din Do Nuttin' (Bodley Head, 1983)
   The Caribbean/British poet, John Agard, draws on memories of Guyana
   as well as life in England in these sparkling poems for younger children.
   Mainly humorous, they touch on the world of children's experience in
   an authentic, yet playful way.
   Say It Again, Granny (Bodley Head, 1986)
   Susanna Gretz is once again the lively illustrator of Agard's poetry. This
   book is based on twenty traditional Caribbean proverbs which the poet
   turns into approachable, dialect poetry. Lots of fun here and wisdom
   too:

   > Say it again, Granny,
   > No rain, no rainbow.

2. Allan Ahlberg
   Please, Mrs Butler (Puffin, 1984)
   Children love these poems. Ahlberg captures school life from the child's
   point of view with humour and sensitivity. I've never known them to fail
   in the classroom.
   Other books to note:
   Each Peach Pear Plum
   Peepo
   Ha Ha Bonk Book
   The last two books are with Janet Ahlberg.
3. Charles Causley
   Figgie Hobbin (Puffin, 1979)
   Perhaps the best of Causley's anthologies for children, it contains many
   of his most popular poems like 'I saw a jolly hunter', 'What happened to
   Lulu?' and 'My mother saw a dancing bear'. Causley is a poet of
   distinction.
   Other books to note:
   The Puffin Book of Magic Verse
   The Puffin Book of Salt-Sea Verse
4. Eleanor Farjeon
   Invitation to a Mouse (Knight Books, 1983)
   Anthony Maitland's illustrations complement Farjeon's gentle rhymes.
   Although some were written as early as 1920, on the whole they are not
   dated and still speak to children today.
   Other books to note:
   The Children's Bells

5. Ted Hughes
   Season Songs (Faber, 1976)
   This book seems to me to reflect the heart of Hughes' poetry: it is vigorous, sensitive and profound. The master word-spinner is at his best in this volume. Poems about animals and nature, always challenging, never conventional.
   Meet My Folks! (Faber, 1961)
   Hughes' crazy and outrageous 'relatives' amuse children greatly.
   Other books to note:
   Ffangs the Vampire
   Under the North Star
   What is the Truth?
6. Roger McGough
   Sky in the Pie (Puffin, 1985)
   A wonderful book of word play, jokes, concrete verse and, of course, poems. The mood is mainly light and zany, but there is plenty to think about too. A must for every junior and middle classroom. Satoshi Kitamura's illustrations are most original and very well suited to the poems.
   Roger McGough and Michael Rosen
   You Tell Me (Penguin, 1979)
   This is a little classic. It contains much that is amusing and memorable. Many of the poems are already firm favourites in primary classrooms. Delightful illustrations by Sara Midda.
7. Gerda Mayer
   The Knockabout Show (Chatto & Windus, 1978)
   A thought-provoking book of poems for the middle age range by Gerda Mayer. Sharp, amusing, at times eccentric, these are poems to stimulate your pupils. Other books to note:
   The Candyfloss Tree with others
8. Adrian Mitchell
   Nothingmas Day (Allison & Busby, 1984)
   A beautiful book to look at, with John Lawrence woodcuts, and a pleasure to read. Although Adrian Mitchell has worked with children over many years, this is his first book of poetry written specially for a younger age group. At times funny, strange, haunting, always rich, these are poems to savour.
9. Judith Nicholls
   Magic Mirror (Faber, 1985)
   Judith Nicolls has a lot to offer children in her first book of poetry. She explores a variety of themes in this slim volume: school life (honest and humorous, the poet used to be a teacher), everyday childhood experiences, a sequence of poems about life in Ancient Egypt. Ranging from the serious and sad to the playful, children will enjoy this book.

10. Gareth Owen
    Song of the City (Fontana Lion, 1985)
    Song of the City won the 1985 Signal Award for Poetry. It was described
    by the judges as 'unselfconsciously contemporary in theme ... solidly
    constructed and traditional in value'. A new collection by Owen has
    been eagerly anticipated since his challenging *Salford Road* out in 1979.
11. *Gargling With Jelly*, edited by Brian Patten (Viking/Kestrel, 1985)
    A refreshingly different anthology, full of wierd and wonderful
    creatures, eccentric and dreadful children, incredible happenings and the
    like, written by Brian Patten, better known as an adult poet and
    performer.
12. Michael Rosen
    Quick, Let's Get Out of Here! (Puffin, 1985)
    This wonderful book is particularly strong in one of Rosen's specialities
    – long, narrative poems, usually hilarious. I rarely manage to get to the
    end of one without bursting out laughing myself. All the poems are true
    to life, fun is never far away, yet there are thoughtful moments too.
    You Can't Catch Me (Puffin, 1982)
    A previous Signal Award winner, this anthology is especially good for
    younger children. Quentin Blake, who is the perfect illustrator for many
    of Rosen's books, surpasses himself with the colourful pictures which
    accompany the poems. Some of the timeless elements of childhood are
    captured here.
    Mind Your Own Business (Fontana Lion, 1974)
    Rosen opened up the world of poetry for children with his inventive
    dramatic monologues, dialogues, running commentaries, word play
    which children love to read and listen to *and* try out for themselves.
    Other books to note:
    Wouldn't You Like To Know
    Don't Put Mustard on the Custard
    That'd Be Telling with J. Griffiths
    When Did You Last Wash Your Socks?
13. Kit Wright
    Rabbiting On (Fontana Lion, 1978)
    Hot Dog (Puffin, 1982)
    I treat these two books together because they both have the same
    flavour. In fact one of the most memorable characters from *Rabbiting
    On*, Dave Dirt, reappears in *Hot Dog*. Lots here to amuse children from
    Wright's laconic pen and Posy Simmonds' jaunty illustrations. Humour
    is uppermost in both books with the poet displaying a sure touch.

Where possible I have indicated the date of the first paperback edition of
each anthology for easy availability.

Appendix 3
Women poets writing for children

In compiling the list of popular poets for children who have published their own anthologies, I was aware of a scarcity of women poets. Although there are many fine women poets writing for younger children, few have their own collections. As teachers are always asking me to suggest good poets, I have compiled a list which I hope will be helpful. This list of women poets includes the following:

• poets writing for children who have not published their own collections, but whose work can be found in general anthologies
• poets with anthologies to their credit which are mainly geared to older readers, but whose work includes some poetry accessible to younger readers
• poets whose collections were published outside the U.K. and are not easily available there

Fleur Adcock	Elizabeth Jennings
Moira Andrew	Amryl Johnson
Patricia Beer	Jenny Joseph
Valerie Bloom	Karla Kuskin
Pauline Clark	Liz Lochhead
Gillian Clarke	Eve Merriam
Ruth Dallas	Lilian Moore
Emily Dickinson	Grace Nichols
Toru Dutt	Sylvia Path
Judith Ellis	Christina Rossetti
Aileen Fisher	Stevie Smith
Rose Fyleman	May Swenson
Phoebe Hesketh	Judith Thurman
Libby Houston	Judith Wright
Patricia Hubbell	

Appendix 4
Some books on teaching poetry

1. *Does It Have To Rhyme?* by Sandy Brownjohn (Hodder & Stoughton, 1980)
2. *What Rhymes With Secret?* by Sandy Brownjohn (Hodder & Stoughton, 1982)

These are very practical books with lots of ideas for tackling poetry. They are popular both with teachers new to poetry, because a lot of guidance is offered, and with experienced poetry teachers as a source of good ideas. There are suggestions of activities for children beginning poetry, word games and the like, as well as quite sophisticated forms and types of poetry explored for more experienced pupils. Rather middle class examples of children's poetry, but the ability of these young writers is impressive.

3. *Catapults And Kingfishers*, by Pie Corbett and Brian Moses (O.U.P., 1986)

   A very practical book on teaching poetry in primary schools. It includes ideas for writing poetry, different poetic 'models', the notion of drafting and many examples of poetry written by children.

4. *Not 'Daffodils' Again!*, edited by K. Calthrop and J. Ede (Schools Council/Longman, 1984)

   One of the last productions by the erstwhile Schools Council. This book is the combined effort of a group of teachers in Nottinghamshire and Derbyshire. It is packed full of accounts of classroom practice, suggestions for 'lessons' with a very useful information section at the end. It is a book that many teachers will find a valuable aid to teaching poetry.

5. *Poetry in the Making*, by Ted Hughes (Faber, 1967)

   In my opinion this is still the best book on children's writing available. I use the term 'writing' advisedly, as Hughes also makes reference to prose. The poet addresses himself directly to the young writer to whom the book is aimed. It grew out of Hughes' involvement with the radio programme. 'Listening and Talking'. I have read it several times and find it fresh and instructive on every reading. Even the language employed to describe the act of writing is rich and vital. The poems used to illustrate each section are well chosen, and tend to be serious and challenging.

6. *Wishes, Lies and Dreams*, by Kenneth Koch (Chelsea House Publications, 1970)

7. *Rose, Where Did You Get That Red?*, by Kenneth Koch (Vintage House N.Y., 1974)

   You won't find these books in many bookshops in this country. They need to be ordered or borrowed from libraries. I include them, because they describe an innovative approach to both reading and writing poetry. Koch is a distinguished American poet himself, and he presents poetry to his young readers in a down-to-earth, yet fascinating way. Good for demystifying poetry.

8. *Teaching Poetry*, by James Reeves (Heinemann, 1958)

   Understanding Poetry, by James Reeves (Pan, 1971)

   How to Write Poetry for Children, by James Reeves (Heinemann, 1981)

   The poet, novelist, teacher and anthologist, James Reeves, wrote three marvellous books about poetry and children. Although a bit dated now, I would still recommend them. Given that his examples are drawn from traditional English poetry and rather conventional, his knowledge of poetry is catholic, and there is still much to learn from this fine poet. *Understanding Poetry* has least to do with children. It is a good primer for basic information on the nature of poetry. The other two have more to offer the classroom teacher.

9. *How Poetry Works*, by Philip Davies Roberts (Penguin, 1986)
   A most interesting book for the teacher who wants to understand poetry better. It is straightforward, very readable and well-informed. Roberts includes a chronological anthology of English poetry which could form a very useful introduction for the non-specialist.

10. *I See A Voice*, by Michael Rosen (Thames/Hutchinson, 1982)
    The well-known poet, Michael Rosen, has written this book with secondary pupils in mind. Once again it has plenty to offer teachers of a younger age group. Like Koch, Rosen is a debunker of myths about poetry. He emphasises the relevance of poetry to the lives of young people today. He focuses on topical issues like war, race, feminism as well as timeless ones like love and friendship. An up-to-date and often hard-hitting choice of poetry is used to illustrate his themes. An essential in the classroom.

11. *Poetry*, by Robin Skelton in the Teach Yourself series (Hodder & Stoughton, 1963)
    If you avoid tackling poetry with children because you feel you don't understand the technicalities, this little book will fill in the background.

12. *The Poet's Manual and Rhyming Dictionary*, by Frances Stillman (Thames & Hudson, 1966)
    A useful work of reference. It contains a large section of rhymed words and chapters on rhythm, rhyme and traditional poetic forms.

13. *Start-Write*, edited by Morag Styles (E.A.R.O., 1986)
    This modest little book provides ideas and strategies for beginning poetry with children. The editor has drawn on the work of twenty Cambridgeshire teachers and their pupils.

The author and publishers are grateful for permission to reproduce the following copyright material in this book:

Dylan Thomas, extracts from *Under Milk Wood*, and 'Fern Hill' from *The Poems*, both published by Dent and reprinted by permission of David Higham Associates Ltd.

Alan Brownjohn, 'Common Sense' from *Sandgrains on a Tray* (1969), published by Secker and Warburg, reprinted by permission of Alan Brownjohn, © Alan Brownjohn.

Robert Frost, 'A Time to Talk' from *The Poetry of Robert Frost*, edited by Edward Connery Lathem, reprinted by permission of Jonathan Cape Ltd. and the Estate of Robert Frost. Copyright 1916, © 1969 by Holt, Rinehart and Winston, Inc. Copyright 1944 by Robert Frost. Reprinted from *The Poetry of Robert Frost*, edited by Edward Connery Lathem, by permission of Henry Holt and Company, Inc.

T. S. Eliot, 'East Coker' from *Four Quartets* in *Collected Poems 1909–1962* reprinted by permission of Faber and Faber Ltd.

E. M. Forster, an extract from 'The Raison D'Etre of Criticism in Art' in *Two Cheers for Democracy*, reprinted by permission of Edward Arnold Ltd.

Ted Hughes, extracts from *Poetry in the Making*, reprinted by permission of Faber and Faber Ltd.

144   *In tune with yourself*

Four Haiku from 'The Bamboo Branch' from *An Introduction to Haiku*, edited by Harold G. Henderson. Copyright © 1958 by Harold Henderson. Reprinted by permission of Doubleday and Co. Inc.
The extract on Haiku by Cathy Pompe comes from *Startwrite* and is reproduced by permission of the publishers, EARO, The Resource Centre, Back Hill, Ely, Cambs CB7 4DA.
Joshua Brown, 'If there were no rabbits' from *Young Writers*, published by Heinemann Educational Books and award-winner in the W. H. Smith Young Writers' Competition 1981, reprinted by permission of W. H. Smith and Son Ltd.
Adrian Mitchell, 'What's that down there?' from *Nothingmas Day*, reprinted by permission of Allison and Busby Ltd.
'You' from *Igbo Traditional Verse* compiled and translated by Romanus Egudu and Donatus Nwoga, reprinted by permission of Heinemann Educational Books.
'Chivy' by Michael Rosen from *You Tell Me* poems by Roger McGough and Michael Rosen (Kestrel Books, 1979), Michael Rosen poems copyright © 1979 by Michael Rosen, collection copyright © 1979 by Penguin Books Ltd.
'The Door' by Miroslav Holub from Miroslav Holub, *Selected Poems* translated by Ian Milner and George Theiner (Penguin Modern European Poets, 1967), copyright © Miroslav Holub 1967, translation copyright © Penguin Books Ltd 1967.
Michael Rosen, 'Down Behind the Dustbin' from *Wouldn't You Like to Know* (1977) reprinted by permission of André Deutsch Ltd.
Rose Fyleman, 'The Goblin', reprinted by permission of The Society of Authors as the literary representative of the Estate of Rose Fyleman.
James Reeves, 'Slowly' and 'The Sea is a Hungry Dog' from *James Reeves, The Complete Poems for Children* by James Reeves, © James Reeves Estate, reprinted by permission of The James Reeves Estate.
T. S. Eliot, extracts from 'Choruses from "The Rock"' and 'Little Gidding' in *Collected Poems 1909–1962*, reprinted by permission of Faber and Faber Ltd.
Terry Jones and Michael Palin, an extract from *Bert Fegg's Nasty Book for Boys and Girls*, reprinted by permission of Methuen London.
Edmond de Rostand, an extract from *Cyrano de Bergerac* translated by Anthony Burgess, reprinted by permission of Hutchinson, as an imprint of Century Hutchinson.
Roger McGough, 'My Week (1)', 'My Week (3)', 'Easy Money', 'Cinema Poem' and 'Haiku' from *Sky in the Pie* by Roger McGough, published by Kestrel Books Ltd. and reprinted by permission of A. D. Peters and Company Ltd.

We would also like to say thank you to those children whose poems have been included in the book: Alex, Clare, Daniel, Fiona, Jamie, Jessica R. Jessica S., Jonathan, Josh, Josh B., Joshua Holmes, Katherine, Libby, Lisa, Luke, Ross, Sophie Ladds, Stuart, Theresa and Zac, who all went to the Homerton Poetry Club; to the children who at the time of writing their poems were at the following schools: Anisa at Arbury County Primary School; Julian at Colville County Primary School; Adam at Histon and Impington County Junior School; the second year junior at Katherine Semar Primary School; Alice, Andrew, Hannah, Harriet, Katherine, Marc, Sarah and Ross at Morley Memorial Primary School; Anna, Jonathan, Satish, Sean at Mayfield Primary School; Camilla, Claire, Joe and Lynne at Park Street Primary School; Jack and Susan at St. Paul's Primary School; Alex and Sophie at Stapleford Primary School; to Catherine Browning, whose address we could not trace, and to those children whose names we could not find, but whose poems are here to be enjoyed by all. Finally thank you to four teachers whose work has contributed to this book: Bernice Wilkinson, Keith Weston, Barbara Oliver and Cathy Pompe, and to EARO for allowing us to use material from *Startwrite* (1986).

Every effort has been made to contact the copyright holders. The authors and publishers would be glad to hear from anyone whose rights they have infringed.